Fred, wishing you every Success and Happiness nothing more then you deserve, in the Truth of who you are! Best Wishes. Geoff.

Solved!

The Truth About Real Success

© Geoffrey J Canavan

GN00357197

© Copyright Information

Published by Time Stop Publications
Product No: TSP0001
ISBN: 978-0-9563082-0-7
©Geoffrey J Canavan 2009
www.geoffreyjcanavan.com

Introduction

Solved! The Truth About Real Success is a book about hope and about rediscovering your lost Self, the Self of perfect success, happiness and harmony.

Like a distant song, we all have a memory of how that perfection feels, but this memory is clouded by what we've learned on our journey through life. Our perception of the world colours all our interactions and how we function on a day-to-day basis. By remembering the perfection of who we are, we can acquire a newfound freedom, a passport to our inherent success.

> We are all born successful but over
> time we learn the art of Self-failure.

By examining how we see the world, how we think and how we act we start to unravel our cycle of failure, Self-doubt and lack of Self-belief.

Sometimes you can catch a hint of your natural state of perfection and success as a vague but not unfamiliar feeling. This book aims to tap into that source and allow you to access the true meaning of who you are.

> Beyond all you see around you shines
> the inner light of your true potential.

This is the golden light of inner belief and inner potential, the distant memory of how you found our way into the world. Everybody will know when you are in tune with your real, perfect and successful Self because that is where we all started.

Whatever aspect of your life you want to focus on, however you define 'success', wherever you want to take that inner perfection, it's really only a matter of realising the unlimited resource that you are and remembering what you have forgotten about your perfect Self.

> Remember, we all start perfectly successful.
> We acquire failure.

Real success is based on who we are within rather than anything we acquire externally. The willingness to look at ourselves in a light of perfection, success, inclusion and determination provides a real opportunity to move forward in the true meaning of peace and happiness.

It starts by simply being prepared to acknowledge and accept the true Self we have forgotten. In that Self is our truth and integrity, where all our interactions and experiences have a meaning of honest and non-fearful expression.

> Every individual recognises the secret
> language of truth. Truth is the universal
> and silent language of integrity.

You don't have to deny your Self. You can look at real alternatives. Now you are being presented with an opportunity to choose again.

Contents

CHAPTER I

Who Are You?

Being Special

Like it or not, our lives are built around other people. We are intricately connected to each other. These connections range from the most superficial to the most intimate. What we learn from our experiences, interactions and connections with other people forms the basis for how we create our judgement and value systems. We assess ourselves and the world around us through these judgement and value systems.

We all have 'special relationships' in love, work, family friends, etc. and how we behave within these situations provides an opportunity to learn about ourselves. We draw on our special relationships to make judgments about ourselves, such as 'how much am I loved?' 'How important am I in my workplace?' 'How valuable am I to my friends?' 'What's my social standing?'

All of our interactions provide the means to evaluate and calculate our role within any situation, from the simplicity of buying a book in a bookstore to the complexity of marrying somebody for life. And so, we learn to form opinions about ourselves and about others and about every situation we meet.

Many facets of life, business, and even the perception we hold of success, are based on the foundation of our special relationships and our judgment. Special relationships can be used to endorse 'I am loved and wanted' or 'I am dismissed and/or unimportant'. So, for example, if I am not invited to the party or I don't get the promotion, I can use my special relationships to evaluate my own worth in a negative sense.

So, rather than getting in touch with our own sense of who we are, we look to our special relationships to define us. Because we are not aware of how special and successful we are in our own right, we clothe ourselves in labels to explain ourselves to the world: I am a Liverpool supporter/a victim/ a musician/an alcoholic/a mother/entrepreneur/bad at maths etc. In truth, we have no need to explain or define ourselves to anyone.

We are all simply perfect.
We are all successful.
We were born that way.

Past Tense

Life has taught many of us to be naturally inclined to gravitate toward the negative, based on what we perceive as failure, loss and isolation. We then use the value we have assigned to our past experiences as a template for future decision-making. When we begin to look beyond the historical negatives we learn that we can choose a more constructive view of the world and not draw exclusively from that sense of being hostage to our past.

As we look at the world slightly differently we start to gain a new sense of freedom that is not limited by an old value system. The secret is to focus on going forward positively without the negative influences of the past.

One failure need not become a life of regret.
Failure in one area does not have to lead to
a world without success.

Teach your Self to value all your experiences and see them as building blocks to where you are now. Even apparent mistakes are educational.

Every experience carries value.

This way of seeing things gives us the chance to use our past in a new way. Now we can focus on learning how we operate rather than judging our perceived lack of performance and continually beating ourselves up with the mantra of 'I can never get it right'.

By constantly referring to my past I limit my Self, which means that I cannot expand my horizons and I will draw more and more on the philosophy of failure.

Bear in mind that we are all born naturally successful, and learn the habit of failure as we grow up. As children we believed we could be, do and have anything we wanted. Where is the little girl who dreamed of being a princess, or the young boy who would be an astronaut?

The real problem is that we tend to use our past as our problem, never really allowing ourselves the opportunity to be all that we are capable of being, never really believing that we are Self-confident and assured in our decision-making. When we overcome that restrictive way of thinking, the sense of freedom is quite extraordinary because always being right doesn't matter any more. Now I know that I make decisions with the belief that I am doing my best. I am working on my future success strategy, rather than from my past fears.

Fear really stifles our ability to achieve, in all aspects of life. Letting go of old fearful influences gives a whole new perspective to how we view our world and as a result the opportunities become much more abundant. Now we're not looking for the problem but, in the knowledge of Self-trust and belief, we embrace the opportunity. Every situation – a global recession, a relationship breakdown, a struggling business, a health challenge - can lead us to a place that doesn't leave us feeling vulnerable and overwhelmed.

> I can be, do and have all I want to be,
> do and have provided I let go of Self-doubt.

Be prepared to see the world and your place within it differently. In other words, envisage the outcome you want and believe that you deserve it and that it can happen. Don't be dogged by your past, regardless of your life experience to date. Now you can face any challenge with a personal freedom from the past. See your Self taking ownership of your right to success.

> Just because I didn't make the grade
> yesterday does not automatically mean
> I won't make it tomorrow.

Identify Yourself

We have all already established an identity. Don't be afraid to let this identity be up for change.

In many instances we find ourselves adapting to situations, almost like being different characters in a play. This gives rise to the many faces of the one person, acting out different roles in different situations, being different things for different people and so often hiding our true Self.

> Success is not about right or wrong.
> It's all about being real.

Even if this reality shows a human vulnerability and an uncertainty it is presenting an opportunity to plug back into the person you deserve to be, which is the successful You.

Sadly, we can all identify much more with what we didn't do than with our achievements. We can (and do) perfect failure. Losing contact with the truth of my Self is the breeding ground where failure is conceived, where fear is born and where vulnerability grows. My true successful Self is never lost but often overshadowed as I live in hope of glimpses of the happiness that some part of me knows I so truly deserve. And so, if I look at my life through the past - where I might have seen my Self as a failure - I find it hard to see a future that includes a really successful Self. That's just human nature but we can change that view

Change begins with awareness and awareness starts from the point of realisation that we are not alone in this fragile human world. Whether you're a king or a pauper, human nature is human nature. Everybody, at some point in their lives, suffers the same sense of inadequacies. Everybody has frailties. This is nothing to hide. It is part of being human and being human is what has us here

When we recognise that we are all starting from the same place we now begin to feel less conscious of our own worries and more open to achievement. The best and most successful of us shares the same insecurity issues as everybody else.

> Success is available to everybody regardless
> of where we started or what happened
> to us along the way.

The opportunity to be all you want to be is waiting. Your belief system and your appreciation of your Self is all it takes to start your journey to being the successful You. Just remember, you were born that way.

Continually remind your Self that success is your right and that you really can be the person you want to be. Be prepared to choose what you want. Refuse to be sidetracked or to allow past failures to dominate your thinking and hold you trapped in a cycle of want. Be open for change.

Inclusion

The whole experience of development and successful growth is not about going it alone and doing it all by yourself. It involves a Self-belief system of inclusion. Inclusion is a huge part of any personal or business development.

Inclusion is simple and simple is successful.

The opposite of inclusion is fragmentation. That's when we all have separate interests and we all take separate views and adopt separate standpoints, which we then feel the need to defend. The label you've attached to your Self - (I am a Liverpool supporter/a victim/a musician/an alcoholic/a mother/an entrepreneur/bad at maths etc) - in order to define who you are within your special relationships and make you feel like you 'belong' actually becomes a weapon that keeps you separated. Fragmentation does not lend itself to coherent growth, development and sustainable planning of life and business.

If my life or my business has primarily functioned on the special relationships I use to define myself and my place in the world, I am limiting myself and compromising my success because my decision-making is coloured by fragmentation, rather than inclusion.

But I can change all that by simply adopting a policy of inclusion and oneness of purpose, where goals are not set in isolation and where opportunities are not mimicked by looking at someone else's apparent success.

> Every relationship of value must have
> a foundation in truth and integrity.

So in other words, we're not going forward from a place of weakness. We're going forward from a place of trust and that trust is really coming from within. We are learning once again to trust ourselves, not based on all that has happened yesterday but with greater emphasis on what is happening now and what we really want to happen tomorrow.

> This self-trust is like a beacon of our own
> acceptance and a statement to the world
> of our entitlement to success.

Out of this comes the expression of how we present ourselves, how we engage with people and how real and valuable interactions happen. Whether it's a conversation with a friend, a sales meeting or important financial discussions when that inner light of looking to be honest is turned on it will be recognised and appreciated.

When we are operating from that place of fearlessness every relationship is special and no relationship is special. We are not threatened, for better or worse, but are functioning in truth and honesty. The foundation of what we're building is incredibly strong and holds great truth, with the purpose of progressing into the future.

> Many people have little faith in themselves
> because they don't realise that success exists
> within and can be brought out by a simple
> change of focus.

See your Self as an achiever, a doer and don't be so hard on your Self. Realise that all your needs can be met - in any area of your life — when you see your Self as you really are, which is 100% acceptable.

Move forward with that depth of awareness that how things were done in the past doesn't have to influence how they are done in the future. Give your Self a clean sheet. Wipe the blackboard. Move beyond history into your future without bringing along your judgments and preconceived notions of the way the world works. Take on board the fact that you have an entitlement and a natural inheritance to successful living and happiness.

CHAPTER 2

The 'I'm Okay Factor'

What You See is What You Get

Perception determines who we are.

Perception is a choice that offers options of how we want to view the world. We can choose to see nothing but a dangerous and frightening world or nothing but a friendly and happy world – or something in between.

Whatever way we decide to perceive the world, we will automatically seek out and always find evidence to support our choice. If I decide that life is a struggle, life will do its best to prove me right. If I decide to view life as an exciting adventure, that's what my life is.

A situation that I consider a big problem you might see as an exciting opportunity - and we will both be right! You might feel that traffic jams provide productive time to listen to some uplifting music or inspirational CDs and I might see them as frustrating, time-wasting nuisances – and we're both right! So my perception of the traffic jam – or any situation – determines how I will experience it.

Perception is my instrument of understanding.

My perception enables me to find reasons to justify my perception. I see the world as dangerous and frightening because .... or I see the world as friendly and happy because ...

Our experience of failure, past or present, has a huge influence on how we actually understand the world and the template that influences our thinking and our decision-making. We can use this template to be Self-motivating or Self-defeating, challenging or inspiring.

It is very easy to use past failures as the main influences on present choices.

Recurring themes of failure are evident when the template of choice remains rooted in a thought system where failure, disappointment and frustration are the main influences. Letting go of the past is a primary step in determining a far more successful and fulfilling future.

> If something you have used consistently
> doesn't work, stop using it. If your past
> template for decision-making is keeping you
> in a limiting loop then stop using that template.

To apply this principle to a relationship of any nature we can look at the recurring theme of failure and then justify it by reasoning why the relationship didn't succeed. We can always find a reason why the business meeting went wrong, why the sale didn't happen, why the love affair ended.

> It is never hard to find tags of failure
> to attach to any situation.

They are usually accompanied by the by-line 'it was not my fault'. This is the common misperception that everything is outside our control and therefore not our fault; all reasoned by our acceptance of failure, based on the decision-making influences that are coming from our past.

I have often heard expressions such as 'knowing my luck, it'll go wrong' or 'if I had ducks, they'd drown'. This becomes an acceptance of 'what can go wrong will go wrong', rather than even an attempt to somehow change old patterns and find a new focus of Self-confidence.

> There is no truth in this 'it's not my fault'
> view because we are taking on board the
> aspect of acceptance without justification,
> which then becomes a substitute for failure.

And so we have a vicious cycle of uncorrected errors where nothing is learned and the only thing we take ownership of is the reason of doubt and the reason of Self-defeat.

On the One Road

You can only think for your Self and when you become aware of how you justify your failure (or your absence of success) it's time to examine how you can correct that (unless you want to stay in the loop of failure, which many people find far more comfortable, because they have become very successful at being a failure).

History repeats at all levels. That's why - in that correction - you have to get away from the idea that we operate separately and accept that we function totally as one entity. Inclusion is a necessary part of success.

Everybody is fighting a hard battle. Everyone faces tough challenges from time to time.

All influences provide an opportunity to look at the world in whatever way we choose, rightly or wrongly, for better or worse. It is so easy to fall into that trap of fearful decision-making, giving rise to separate interests with separation being our experience. This feeds further separation and further isolation where our true potential as a person of inclusion, success and acceptance cannot surface and stops us becoming the success we want to be.

Taking ownership of your own success is crucial, even if all you can manage now are the first baby step of having the willingness to wake up one day and say 'yes I want to break this cycle and I am prepared to somehow try to see my world from a different perspective. I want to stop the Self defeat and I can start today'.

Clichéd as it may sound, today really is the first day of the rest of your life. Inspire your Self in the knowledge and belief that you can create a different world than the one you have come to know.

> Be fearless in your choice to find your
> own freedom. Do not put a value on the
> invaluable Self that is You. Invaluable means
> no limitations. Value sets a limit. Be priceless
> in your own Self-worth.

You do not leave Self-doubt by bringing it to somewhere else. There is no somewhere else. You leave it by simply understanding the power of your ability to choose.

> You have the right to choose happiness.

Simple and straightforward, this is the powerful key to unlocking your world of abundance. Unrestricted, you can make that decision right now. Freedom is yours without constraint. View your world with as much understanding as possible and realise that you choose to experience the world you want.

> Failure is forgetting to remember the
> opportunities you can give to your Self.

Win-Win

This does not mean that every situation we encounter will result in monetary, personal or social gain, or whatever perception of success we may have. It means that, even where the situation doesn't look like it's working out, we recognise the opportunity for a successful learning process and it does not become an attack or an endorsement of separation, isolation and fear.

You don't have to buy into that eternal loop of Self-criticism, Self-doubt, fear and removal from the truth.

Instead, whatever the outcome, use every situation as a learning opportunity. In your day-to-day experience, the goal is to make success continuous.

Learn to be less accepting of failure and have a greater openness to success. You don't have to see your Self without hope. Nothing is ever hopeless. Teach your Self to be as you would want your Self to be. See your Self as somebody you would aspire to admire and somebody you would value for their honesty, integrity and Self-belief.

Resolve to not be afraid or fearful or overly occupied with the outcome of any situation in life. If your focus is on being in a place of happiness with your Self, then that's all that matters, not based on third party opinion, but with the realisation that 'I am becoming the me I want to be.' In viewing the world this way, you start to see real opportunities and you're now giving your Self a real chance to finally say

'I'm okay. I'm a work in progress,
but guess what, I'm okay'.

Acknowledging your 'I'm Okay Factor' is where all success begins. Now you're taking the weight of the world off your Self because you're taking steps towards joining life, not in fear, but in true Self-expression, with a true purpose and a much greater acceptance of who you are. You are becoming 'the fearless me'.

So now the world becomes a university
teaching you the value of your Self and
not a fearful place.

The way you see the world becomes the world you want to see. Start to see your Self as the Self you want to be. Being free comes from your perception of freedom. Being successful comes from your perception of success. We all get trapped in perception - our perception of strength, our perception of weakness.

Success only requires that your acceptance
of your inherent right to success is stronger
than your acceptance of your sense of failure.

Be For You

Begin each day by realising that you are for your Self. Be powerful in the presence of who you really are and what you want to be. Align your Self with your birthright, which is success. Fear comes from feeling inadequate and it's quite natural for all of us to feel this way. It doesn't mean that you are inadequate and it doesn't mean you can't control those feelings, but you can liberate your Self by knowing how you work. Powerless you are not. Inadequate you never were.

Success has more to do with how you see the world, how you see your own circumstances and how you change your perception of what you see.

> You can attract success just as easily as you can attract failure.

Don't lose sight of being practical and using common sense without agendas, without the complications from past experiences.

Wanting to change something in life or business is the beginning of opening the door of possibility. The opportunity for change is conceived in the wanting to change and born from the willingness to change. Remember that it is only as you look, you learn.

Overcoming apparent difficulties is all part of the learning. Assessing the difficulties and seeing them from a different perspective presents you with the opportunity to change.

> Because something was difficult to overcome
> in the past doesn't mean it has to be like that
> in the future.

All you're doing is breaking a cycle and re-engaging from a place of inclusion as opposed to focusing all your attention on the separateness of the situation.

Eventually it becomes a natural process. Then your reason and your ability to make decisions and then your justification starts to change, gradually at first, more easily as you proceed.

> Eventually every day is a day of opportunity
> and every day is an experience of success,
> bearing in mind the need to be gentle with
> your Self and patient with the process.

Find the Lesson

My brother was diagnosed with cancer in May. By June he had passed away.

Initially the situation was one of horror, shock, sadness and anger but as we went through the weeks and as his failing health became more evident, we also realised that anything we needed to talk about would have to be done sooner, rather than later.

One afternoon, we drove to the countryside and, even though he was very weak, with great determination my brother climbed a small hill that gave us a wonderful view of the surrounding world. We sat there for 3 hours and spoke of almost every life story we had engaged in together.

When the time came to leave, we both knew that my brother was returning to the hospital to die, but in the sadness of the situation could not bring ourselves to speak of his pending journey.

We stood up from where we'd been sitting and in simultaneous, spontaneous action, hugged each other and cried like two lost souls.

> Words had failed us, but emotion and the
> true language of who we are spoke in volumes.

We stood there crying and holding each other's broken hearts; broken in the knowledge that on the face of it, we were soon to be parted, although in truth he has always remained never more than a thought away.

I got to know my brother and my Self that day in a way that was more beautiful than any brother-to-brother experience I can describe. It was true. It was unconditional and, like two columns of light, we intertwined in the wonderment of showing each other just how much we cared.

If any good was to come from the tragedy of losing somebody to cancer then the journey of enlightenment I experienced that day was a direct result of where we both found ourselves in the stories that were our lives.

> Out of the darkest of places can emerge
> the brightest of lights, leading to a knowledge
> and a freedom that is far more than the
> transient nature of anyone's life.

When I embraced my brother that day amidst tears and sadness I also embraced my Self in the hope and truth that, as we see ourselves losing something, we can also see ourselves finding a truth we may have thought we had lost.

I try not to say in sadness how much I miss him. I rather think how this situation gave both of us an opportunity to learn so much of the truth of who we are and the truth of life itself.

Not every situation is as dramatic as the death of a family member and not every situation will carry such profound emotion, imagery, messages and often enlightenment, but there is no doubt that as we go through life every experience gives us the chance to reassess our decision-making process, our judgments and our opportunities for correction. Correction gives us choices of how we want to live and how we want to see ourselves.

With or without drama, we can make that change from that wayward place of loss, vulnerability and indifference to a world which is ours in all its completion. Dramatic circumstances are often a wake up call to change direction and reassess the immediate nature of who we are.

> Learn to make decisions without the drama
> from that heart-felt place where you want to
> give your Self the truth and the meaningful life
> that you know you deserve.

Sometimes, a perceived loss is not that at all. Every situation is only a loss when you fail to learn a little bit more about the truth and human frailty that we all are. When you close your Self to learning then you open your heart to loss. This becomes the sadness of the forgotten child within each and every one of our hearts. Find the child and give him or her love and opportunity truly deserved, the love that's there to find in every single story that makes up our lives.

CHAPTER 3

What Are We Really Afraid Of?

Who's Got the Power?

When we fear something we are handing our personal power over to that which we fear. When we're afraid of circumstances, situations or loss, we're really giving our power away to the circumstance, situation or the loss.

> What you fear has no power until you
> give it yours.

So, whether we're facing health issues, the bank manager, a hungry tiger or an uncertain tomorrow, we only become powerless when we surrender our power.

Our belief systems are based on our values. When fear enters the equation it really tests those values and becomes the catalyst that can ultimately destroy our options and our ability to achieve success.

If we're basing our decision-making on past, negative experiences we tend to escalate our need for defensiveness. As we build our defences we also build the barriers that keep us rooted in failure.

> So we create our defences, we make them
> seem extremely real and that then becomes
> our world.

This defensiveness becomes the model we use to determine how we conduct our engagements. So if we're heading to that meeting or if we're discussing aspects of growth and development in business or relationships, we are using a template that is rigidly set on the Self-protecting patterns we have established.

It is very important to look at the defence mechanisms we use, how we justify them and what beliefs have shaped them.

> Understanding why we are defensive is
> not difficult. Life teaches us all to be that way.

Self-protection and Self-preservation are key factors in personal growth. We learn (often the hard way) not to stick our fingers in the fire, run across the road without looking both ways, jump out of a second story window, fall madly in love with movie stars or spend more than we earn.

It is very easy to justify the dynamic of Self-protection and Self-preservation, particularly when we witness such day-to-day tragedies. They surround us in every media - print radio, television, the internet - on a 24/7 basis. Because we are constantly being exposed to that currency of fear - from health issues to personal security to the global economic crisis - it's quite understandable how our natural defensiveness becomes heightened and sometimes greatly misguided.

> An example of misguided defensive thinking
> is seeing yesterday as failure, today as blame
> and tomorrow as fear.

This is something we can all slip into with great ease because many of us believe we have had failed yesterday's and look forward to fearful tomorrows. As we hold on to this thought pattern, our identity becomes rooted in the past. The limitation of the future seems now to be the norm when in truth there is no limitation and the real challenge is rising above the past, making the future an abundant successful zone where you can be whatever you want.

The instinct to protect your Self is not a
failing or a weakness.

It is a fact. But when we use Self-protection and Self-preservation disproportionally to make decisions, the fact can become a limiting factor that distorts our judgment and causes us to shut down to the world, rather than opening up to our full potential.

Success is nothing more, and should be
seen as nothing more, than an inherent
part of your life.

It is your right to be the successful You, you already are. All that separates you and your better future is the habit of using your past as the only yardstick to how you live. Letting the past go and not enslaving your Self is your real ticket to freedom. Don't just be the You you want to be, but be the You you deserve to be.

Success is your inheritance. It is rightfully
yours. Failure is an acquired skill.

Inside Out

The past got us to where you we now but that doesn't mean that our present has to decide our future. The external circumstances of our world do not determine the kind of person internally we are.

Everybody has a choice for change. Make your choice in the knowledge that you can be in a far better place by not bringing a paralysing past life to all your ideas around what your future should look like. Be strong in the belief that you now have opportunity. Take ownership of your future with a successful template of how you would see it acted out.

Your future is yours just as much as your past.

Own it, love it, live it.
Don't see your Self marginalised and stop comparing your Self to others. Their failure or their success has no bearing on what you can be by your own choice and desire. Be more conscious of the limitless nature of your very existence.

Turn on the tap of Self-abundance that really comes from within. Like switching on that light, you can let the world see your potential to shine.

Without agendas, this natural recognition will reveal who you want to be and then your world responds accordingly. Truth loves truth. Success loves success. We can't but admire the honesty of somebody turning on the light of who they are and who they should be.

The radiance of you wanting to be a better You is immense.

In every engagement and all facets of your life this turned on light of Self becomes evident, recognised and admired. It's like moving up a gear in your interactions as you bring a new energy and freshness to what you're doing.

You are now teaching your Self that you can give your Self a future - just as the world that you have experienced has given you a past - only this time the future is far more influenced by the You you have decided to be, the You of completion and success.

A friend of mine once said 'if things don't change around here they'll stay exactly the same' and he's right! Your first change comes from your decision about your future and how you want your world to be. Make that change.

It doesn't matter where you are now or the seeming futility of your situation.

There is always an opportunity for newness.

There is always an opportunity to choose a different perspective on a seemingly same and contained life. Even within business the biggest boost you can offer to any company is that of bringing the dynamic of change and engagement. Parallels exist in all walks of life - families, love affairs, hobbies. This simple shift of perspective has such a huge impact that most people are totally surprised by the vast difference a small adjustment to the thinking process can make to their experience of life.

Bring out your own brilliance as you learn to appreciate, trust and value the objective of being the better You.

Into the Future

It's really simply a process of breaking the cycle and saying 'I can change all of this for the better' in a final determination to see your Self as being alright. Stay in touch with your I'm Okay Factor and lose that sense of a lost life or a hopeless dilemma. Regardless of where you feel you are now, each one of us has an inherent ability to tap into the creative resource that becomes our 'out of the past. into the future' system.

> Becoming aware of a pattern of repeated
> mistakes in your past enables you to recognise
> the need and want for a more determined and
> fulfilling present and future.

Recognise your Self for who you really are. Avoid being excessively harsh in criticising your Self or others around you. The secret is to stop, reassess and move on with determined Self-engagement. This time make the journey yours.

Remember, you have the ability already within. It is a built-in mechanism, born by the essence of your very creation. Finding it is nothing more than making the decision to acknowledge its existence and, when you acknowledge that, you set out on the road to completion of your Self and your capabilities. This leaves you totally un-wanting and free to express your Self. Agenda-less relationships and life become a freedom. Knowledge becomes truth and truth stimulates a growing recognition of that same truth in others.

In other words, as we learn admire the good in ourselves we recognise, appreciate and admire the same qualities in others.

As you grow in this process of Self-recognition you also find a new determination that allows you to work, live and function with much greater ease. It all comes from that inner sense of 'the great new me', bringing a freshness and more importantly, an honest vibrancy to what you once viewed as old and tired situations. It's like letting your mind out of jail and allowing your Self a super freedom with new horizons.

I am unlimited and I was born free and so, in all I do, my awareness of my unlimited Self will be my foremost presence.

One step at a time, I learn to move into this space; not rushed, not panicked but in the gentle knowledge that I am determined to travel in this new and right direction.

So now, when faced with apparent difficulties or what could be thought of as frightening situations, stop and ask your Self 'can I see this differently? Where is my sense of Self worth to be found? Where is my power?'

Let your belief in your own innate success speak for you, in any situation.

Then the world will start to recognise that your light of Self-determination is well and truly on. The start of being seen for who you really are and what you can be is very evident and, in that great willingness to be free of the past, you begin to see your Self for everything you are.

The liberation has begun.

CHAPTER 4

Breaking
the Loop

Step off the Treadmill

Being really successful is about mining the potential of who you are and what you can do. Achieving this success is a great expression of your Self. It is a real natural process and a real unveiling to the world of the true You.

> Nobody is born a failure but our attraction
> to the failed process or the failed anything, can
> become an addiction.

We can choose to keep going back to where we are imprisoned by our own belief system and by our own attachment to loss and to fear and ultimately to failure. This loop automatically repeats itself until we choose differently. Just look around and you will see that so many of us are attracted to recurring bad situations, as if to give up on our natural birthright of success.

Within the loop of limitation it becomes very hard to step outside that cycle, particularly as we are so conditioned by our day to day commitments; 'I have to work, I have to take care of the kids' 'I have to organise the meeting' etc. The 'I Have to Syndrome' is a bit like a treadmill; it is difficult, but not impossible, to stop. Stopping necessitates seeing your Self correctly and not just as a victim of the 'I Have to Syndrome'.

Success is never about what you are doing, where you work, where you live, who your friends are, how much you earn or how your life looks. It is always about how you see your Self in any given situation.

These are the situations that make up the world that surrounds you and the world that surrounds you allows you to make judgments about how you function and how you want to be. Your reaction is always based on your Self-value so, in assessing the loop of life, you must assess your Self. Are you on that treadmill and if so, how can you change or give your Self the opportunity to live a little differently?

Learn to look at the world from the perception of your own success. However that may appear, it is yours.

Trust with a Capital T

Success comes from the mind that is ready for it but for many of us 'I would but …' becomes the cop out and then the excuse department is endless. Failure can have addictive qualities all built from the loop of personal history. When we get good at not achieving we can perfect the art of not achieving.

Some of us can make a lifestyle out of repeating the same mistake over and over and over. I have known some of the most successful failures in the world.

> The addiction to the failed Self is as strong as any addiction there is.

So now let's look at trusting that you are ready for success and then doing something about it. Trusting gets you out of that loop. It is vital to really Trust your Self (with a capital T) and access that inner feeling that you can be more. Believe and you shall be.

> Trust that there is an inner You capable of great achievements.

As you trust, your belief in the trusting process starts to dismantle fears, anxieties and what you may have perceived as threats; all of the things that would have kept you separate from the world you want.

Trust allows you to push out boundaries in the belief and knowledge of your own personal capabilities. Start giving your Self the opportunities to be and watch out for the trap of 'I would but…'.

Look around you at those you could call 'icons of greatness', and realise that the attractive quality they seem to possess – charisma, presence, confidence – has come from within. It's not something they have bought. It's not something that they have taken from somebody else. It has come exclusively from within each person.

> This aura or personal presence is the coming together with your Self in that place where you're actually ready to accept your Self as successful.

It is so easy to witness the success quality in others and yet be slow to accept it in ourselves. This just illustrates how hard it can be to start the correction of Self-acceptance.

Poor Me!

Beware the constant attraction that all of us carry to feel hard done by and the subsequent feelings of how unfair the world can be that become a hiding place from the more fulfilling journey of achievement.

I learned the truth of how we identify with this loop when, on many occasions, my own personal sense of isolation reminded me just how unconnected we can allow ourselves to become.

For example, I once worked on a significant distribution deal with a large company that was chaired by a good friend of mine. This was a major national distribution agreement. Convinced I had been awarded the contract, I delighted in my ability to make this happen. Lots of time, effort and energy went in to securing the deal. From my perspective, the opportunities for both our companies seemed obvious; we could deliver the service and they had the product that needed delivering.

The hallmark throughout the negotiations hinged on my relationship with some key executives from the other company. I felt from an early stage that this was a done deal. All we had to do for the final round of negotiation was to sign on the dotted line. When the decision on the contract was announced I was surprised, amazed and disappointed that my company hadn't actually got it.

My initial reaction was one of disbelief and then annoyance. All that work and effort to no avail. However, the real prize within this apparent rejection whereby we seemed to have been totally led up the garden path was that now I had an opportunity to examine and appraise the relationships and boundaries within my working practice.

This apparent rejection presented me with
the option of looking at the way I did business
and the chance to view the situation as a
classroom and not as a defeat.

In a roundabout way, it was a perfect example of people attempting to achieve success built on specialness, rather than on the integrity of the process. One of my big lessons was to look at the agendas I carry into this type of transaction and, for that matter, into all my interactions. In this instance the intent was not one of inclusion, it was far more to do with the individuals involved serving separate interests.

As I've said before, inclusion is a fundamental element of success. From the outset, establish the limitations and deal with them and in that dealing start to see that the only limitation is your own belief in how you limit your Self.

Success is not about whether you get the
contract or sign that deal or win the lottery
or find the perfect partner. It has far more
to do with honest assessment and appraisal.

Putting the clearest and most honest picture you can as the main agenda gives you a chance to see any situation as it really is and not complicate it through skewed judgments based on past experience or misguided notions of what the other person might do or want.

Be true to your Self in any situation and learn
how capable you can be in establishing a future
success pattern, uncomplicated and secure.

I had so much opportunity to reflect on how unfairly treated I had been that I could have spent years of wasted time wallowing in the perceived failure and betrayal when in essence what I was really being given was a splendid opportunity to recognise that my own Self-worth far exceeded any distribution deal or any special friendships. What I really should have done was written to the company and my friend to thank him for illuminating my own personal value to my Self.

As said before, beware the temptation to feel unfairly treated. Misery loves company.

R.E.S.P.E.C.T.

Life gives us so many opportunities to steer a direction or to plot a course. In many instances we choose to complicate this process by mindless compromising of our own Self-value.

It's not about who wins. Life is about our perception of being a winner. Even if you don't come first you can still hold winner status in your own personal journey.

This is far more important than winning at any price, particularly if it necessitates compromising. Believe me; every one of us will know when we have compromised to the point of Self loss.

Success doesn't have a size.
Success has a realisation.

Stop hiding your Self from opportunities through a history of empty communication. The story of the distribution deal is a great example of empty communication. Nobody involved put a real value on truth and Self worth and so we engaged in a dance of illusion, playing to the ego nature of our humanity and dealing with everything but the truth, which inevitably came to the fore eventually.

There is a great abundance in truth. It's almost like giving your Self back to your Self or rediscovering a real inner honesty that carries incredible power, complete and perfectly fine.

> Nobody ever started life with the intention
> of making themselves a failure but, if your
> world is filled with a lack of Self-union, then
> it becomes an easy option to keep functioning
> as the successful failure you know you're not.

Through purpose and fullness you can break that repeat pattern of empty communication and restore the Self-respect you so richly deserve. By respecting your Self you automatically come to respect others and hence the way you interact and the outcome of your day-to-day relationships evolve to a new level.

Hold That Thought

So now in seeing life as a journey, you start to realise that you have protection from this cycle. You now start to look at how you make decisions and how you make choices, how you take your Self forward and how you start to teach your Self that holding the true nature of who you are – which is successful – is the main condition for your engagement at all levels. Do this and watch the change.

Even one day of holding the thought of your personal non-judgmental innocence and success for future endeavours becomes a stepping stone whereby an unyielding future can begin to be unravelled, without compromising the truth of who you are and with the acceptance that everybody fights the very same hard battle of anxiety and doubt.

> Regardless of apparent success, fame or fortune everybody, just by human nature, will at some point experience the grip of Self-doubt.

By seeing your Self truthfully, competent and whole, you start to see others - regardless of difference - in that same frame. We are all striving to overcome the same difficulties, which simply amount to nothing more than being human and recognising it.

> With greater Self-love you can now see your world, not so much as a place where you are held but more as a classroom of Self-fulfilling completion, an adventure of fun and not fear.

Your Choice

There is a choice in terms of your decision-making here and that choice is yours alone. You can choose emptiness, which is simply paralysing your Self and reducing all forms of creativity to almost nothing. That emptiness then becomes a smokescreen in front of your true potential, which is always intact. It's just a matter of having the confidence to show it.

Or you can choose the opposite to the fear by engaging without agendas in the knowledge that, regardless of where you are right now, you have an alternative which does not limit your true potential and is based on the fairness of who we all are and where exploitation or taking advantage is not part of the process.

In other words, the fairness and understanding you show your Self becomes the fairness and understanding you show others and, ultimately, the fairness and understanding the world will show you.

Then every situation and everybody is coming from a position of equality. When you go to your next meeting, in terms of a practical example, realise that - regardless of inner feelings, regardless of previous experience - there is now a decision to make and that's a decision that's made on equality, an equality of purpose, an equality of place.

So now you're giving your Self an assurance as opposed to a warning. This consistency creates the status of truthfulness. Truth is eternal and cannot be changed and now within that process - where you have broken the loop - you have ultimately increased the stability and the ability going forward. We learn this by virtue of the fact that we want to learn it. Be optimistic and give your Self a chance, as opposed to giving your Self one more reason for staying trapped.

> Always remember that lack does not exist in the creation of success. The only sense of lack within your Self that you need to correct is the lack of success that you may have felt.

Vision

In a unified **Self** we have more direction and greater presence, a presence to be perceived in how you live your life. Holding your unity is taking ownership of the greatness and potential you can offer to your own day-to-day world. But once again it's all about how you start that process of recovery; that process of making choices and allowing your **Self** the opportunity for change. What you're really doing here is stopping the process of **Self**-denial because that only results in illusions.

Relating to your world and the people within your world will never come from anything external. The vision of your Self is the vision you make up from within. It will always come from what the kind of person you see your Self as.

> So it is essential that you see the real vision of your Self and not the distorted glimpse based on your history and your fears.

Anything you do that comes from a distortion is really only a misrepresentation of what you are. See the clarity of life, the truth of life and the potential opportunities of living your life to the fullest.

Avoid becoming a slave to the warped view of your own abilities and capabilities and rather embrace the wonderful You with all your talents and potential.

Everyone can contribute at some level.
Be the person you want to be.
You will be admired and seen.
Switch on the light that says 'I am here'.

Learning this process requires some attention and some work. As you grow through it, you will become better at recognising where you get caught up and this recognition presents the opportunity to change and to do so without fear. Watch out for repetition; most of us make the same mistakes repeatedly.

If you start to see your Self as equal in every situation then there is nothing to fear. There is no sense of awe at what you're trying to achieve, which is really staying in touch with your purposeful nature. This then in turn gives you the ability to live out that success that you so deservedly desire.

Learning to like your Self makes
you want to like your Self more.
Self-belief is your passport to Self-freedom.

There are endless opportunities to go through the process of Self-discovery and the rediscovery of your world and the people in it. All you need is the willingness and the rest becomes simple. In essence, you're just getting in contact with the truth of who you are, once again reminding your Self that you started life in a state of perfection, successful and complete.

Apply the process of looking again and realising that you have choices in your day-to-day experiences. Watch the changes as that silent language of success becomes apparent, as you gradually start to see your own capabilities come to the surface.

Success is like knowledge; the more you
have the easier the questions become
so stay focused on the realisation that
you can succeed.

This is where there is no neediness, no want, just effective Self-communication and expression and presence. The truth resonates and the best possible outcome will be decided upon in the knowledge that you are growing. The application of your achievement takes purpose and meaning for your Self. You are becoming all you ever wanted to be in the knowing that you can.

Learn

The following story is an illustration of how sometimes circumstances, when they present to us, give us an opportunity to reflect on where we are and to choose once again how we want to live.

Having run a very large business, employing close to a hundred people and turning over many millions, I found myself in a situation where the business no longer existed and my job as I had known it no longer existed. I had received many accolades in terms of what I had done, but the business failed.

I needed to earn some income and so I opened a video rental store. It was a complete change from what I had done in the previous years and it certainly didn't have the heights of television appearances, newspaper articles and all the other furniture of the world of a high-profile, successful company.

One day while working in the store a guy came in to return the newly released James Bond movie. This was long before downloading or the world of high tech so the release of a James Bond movie was hugely significant in terms of the video rental business.

When I saw what he was returning, just to make conversation, I asked if it was any good, to which he replied, 'it was, but it was very hard to believe in places.'

I was about to explain that the film wasn't actually portraying a true story, nor was it a documentary, when I realised that this was more a reflection of where I was than where he was. It was a great illustration to me that it was about time that I moved on and made the decision to change my circumstances.

> We all have the freedom to choose so
> we shouldn't restrict ourselves in situations
> where we get glaring illustrations of how
> we're compromising, undervaluing or
> limiting ourselves.

That's the time to take the opportunity to look again at where you are and to make some decisions in right-minded-fullness of what you want to do and more importantly, who you want to be.

Be Kind

If you can understand that your natural instinct is to be far more Self-critical than is really necessary then that gives you a foundation to start the reconstruction of your mindset for personal achievement and more successful living.

Most of us assume the worst without ever asking ourselves why because we instinctively take ownership of Self-doubt and shortcomings within any situation.

The focus of understanding how to change this instinctive behaviour starts by learning to see the journey as one step at a time, as opposed to wanting a huge instantaneous shift, subsequently failing and then ending back at the beginning laboured with doubt one more time.

Be gentle with your Self but remain focused in the awareness that there is another way, a way of positive truth and Self-fulfilment.

Life's journey is not about avoidance. It's about engagement and abundant reward. As you see it, you live it.

By starting to see the inner perfection you automatically experience a better world around you.

CHAPTER 5

Starting Over

Stuck!

As we look back over our past, we inevitably see certain patterns. Everybody has this experience and everybody at some point justifies the repetitive nature of their decision-making. Within that pattern process we now have an opportunity to focus on change and break the mould of repeat personal history and end the cycle which in truth has been a personal injustice for so long. Stepping forward as opposed to looking back, that's really our aim.

> It is always so much easier to recognise
> and solve other people's problems than
> to deal with our own.

We can recognise the repeat pattern of apparent disaster in other people's lives, such as the woman who marries the wife beater and leaves him for another man who is equally abusive. Staying in a destructive relationship is an endorsement of the hopelessness that a person feels about themselves and how, trapped and lost, they try to find some value to the tragedy that their life has become. For all parties concerned there is nothing of integrity in the immediacy and intimacy of the pain. Scared and diminished by life circumstances, it is hard to find a window of escape or opportunity, or so it would appear.

Not only in the brutality of physical abuse – which is extreme - do we witness hopelessness but also in the war of psychological abuse. This takes so many forms; the quiet desperation of an unhappy life, the unfulfilled dreams and the diminished hope of sad and disappointed people. Here also is the same sense of lost innocence. Not knowing how they got there, they struggle to re-find and refresh something of their former being. Destroying the beauty that was once the love, saddened and accepting, they let go in freefall of emotional disbelief. Life holds no more enchantment, no truth, only a bitterness born out of lost Self-belief. We all know examples where people feed this sadness from a history of disappointment accepting so many shortcomings and compromises in their struggle to just get by and survive.

Any area of life can become a place that perpetuates Self-destruction, a frontier of renewed and recurring un-fulfilment. It is in this situation that you can move from bad to worse, more a magnet for denial and unhappiness than anything else. Change seems increasingly impossible as people create reasons and justifications for why they have to accept being stuck or trapped.

When your life experience is generating huge pressures then it's increasingly difficult to engage the first steps of choice or to decide to look at life slightly differently. That block keeps you trapped and enslaved on an ongoing basis. Many people will readily admit to feeling that change is beyond their own control and to this end do very little to begin the endeavour for difference. Horror holds us in horror and, gripped in our day-to-day difficulties, a sense of stagnation and forced isolation permeates our world. Repetition is a huge part of the continuum of unhappiness.

Some people consistently make bad career choices and yet have perfectly happy marriages. On the other hand, you'll see the exact opposite where success is abundant in someone's career and yet they can be starved of real meaning and satisfaction in their personal lives. This doesn't mean that you have to trade one against the other.

You can have it all if you can bring your awareness to see that the true You is a completed You and not a partially successful You.

> Go for it all and don't be afraid to want it all,
> not just half the story. As I keep saying,
> it's your right. Learn to own what is yours.

Change

We all find areas where we can really compromise ourselves. We perfect that process and those patterns and it becomes second nature in how we live and what controls our lives. We repeat the same mistakes in the same areas over and over again, keeping us trapped and un-free as the apparent shackles of our existence hold us in a pattern of frustration, confusion and unclear destiny.

But opportunities for change are always present. Replace the sadness with an addiction to the successful You, regardless of circumstances. Find the successful You, which is within all of us, and bring him or her home.

> Not one of us was born to fail or to exist
> in misery or as some form of a lost cause.
> Our birthright is one of growth, fulfilment
> and completion.

Stay focused on your objective of finding and being the best You you can be and don't be overwhelmed if at any point the task seems enormous. Stick to the 'one step at a time' philosophy and what starts as a slow walk will soon be a fast run to more successful living.

It is essential for the purpose of success and fulfilment that you don't set limits, because what is limited then becomes a yardstick to limit your Self. If, in all your relationships, your work, your personal life - whatever aspect you care to look at – you don't blame others, or don't constantly put the problem outside of your Self, you are allowing your Self to go forward in a very creative and fulfilling way that's not shackled by a feeling that the world is out to get you. In essence, you're taking responsibility for your life in a more caring and loving way and creating a reality of completion where now your Self-fulfilling disasters can become your Self-fulfilling joys. You are free from the notion that you can't control your own destiny.

> Everybody has felt lost or shipwrecked
> at some stage of their life.

If you can imagine your Self as a child lost on a journey and then see yourself as the person you are now finding that child and bringing your Self home, then you begin to appreciate the need for Self-understanding on what can be a difficult path but should never be a hopeless one.

> What can be more unjust than denying
> your Self the right to be your Self?

It is a futile exercise to keep your Self held in this place where your true function can never be fully realised.

> Your true function is not a failed function.
> Your true function is to understand that
> personal fulfilment is derived from tapping
> into that source of Self which you know is
> not failed, flawed or diminished.

Be the beautiful person you are (and if you smile as you read this, make sure your smile is sincere, not cynical!).

When we let go of our fear of failure (or success) we really clear the way to be successful. It's like a fog lifting and giving us an opportunity to be visionary.

Don't fear the future. See it for what you want it to be - a successful future without fear. Focus on one step at a time and on your willingness to break the cycle of what was the essence of your past.

> Take every day as an opportunity to
> change and to create the life you want.

And Now

By making the **N**ow your domain of success you can actually go on to achieve what you truly deserve and what we all truly want. Who, for example doesn't want to succeed or doesn't want to be successful? Even when you don't understand the situation or circumstances there is an opportunity to educate your **S**elf once again about your perception and not buy back into that vicious circle of attack.

Sometimes understanding everything just isn't possible. There has to be an acceptance of the journey you are on and the possibilities that arise in this trip of discovery. Everything happens in the Now.

> You can only live in the present,
> not the past, not the future.

Being aware of this becomes a great guide to seeing a less futile world and a less fearful life.

See how much letting go you can actually do and how much of your historical thought processes that you call upon.

> Let go of that cycle of the failure of
> yesterday, the anxiety of today and
> the fear of tomorrow.

There is no fear of tomorrow; there is just the acceptance of Now as part of that process of your development.

In educating your Self to do this you must look with a degree of patience and a degree of calm. It's not something that's going to happen overnight. What can happen instantly is your willingness to look at every situation slightly different, which offers you freedom and a composed purposefulness going forward.

> Wanting to change becomes the first
> step of change itself.

Every encounter now can have a different meaning and can present a different opportunity. Your everyday interactions become your building blocks to get you to the place where your Self-imposed injustice is ending and your true success unfolds. You really are teaching your Self to disempower the old ideas of how life should be and you are getting much more in touch with the new idea of how you will arrive at the life you want. After all, remember it is your life.

Within apparent failures you recognise the opportunity for growth and learning and that becomes the essence of your success. Out of what appears to be a needless failure, there becomes reason and sense as opposed to bitterness, distraction, confusion.

Every encounter becomes a lesson in opportunity and so Self-recognition replaces Self-deception. Believing your Self to be a failure is Self-deception. You are in essence a success.

> Even if you have deviated from your
> success-focussed path, the core of what
> you are is successfulness itself.

With this view you enter a place of truth and honesty and a more grounded place of development. It's like you're learning a new structure and a new form in which you will conduct your life and business. You won't be sidetracked by Self-indifference or Self-persuasion leading to repeated failure.

> Look differently, see differently and start
> to live differently and begin to unravel
> the simplicity of success.

Be mindful of your Self on this journey and what you want for your Self. Hold onto that idea of where you see your Self and where you want to be.

If you were asked 'is this the life you'd want for your children?' make sure that the answer is 'yes'. Make sure that you can attain that fulfilment you so deserve. The end of the injustice is there for you. Make sure you're not afraid to embrace it. Make sure you're not afraid of letting go what you've historically known your Self to be, what you've known your career to be.

Take the simple first step of being prepared to look and then watch the difference as it unfolds. That willingness ignites the process whereby the whole shift, the whole emphasis of what you do and how you do it, begins to take place.

> All you need is the willingness, nothing else.

So have that readiness and have that fearlessness towards your own future, toward your own deserved achievements in truth and toward getting to that place in life that you actually deserve.

Your new life is born from the realisation that you are fundamentally okay and that you are worthy of being where fulfilment and happiness are yours. It all starts when you realise that there are choices and there are other ways to live.

> Meet your Self on your own journey home.
> That home is one of success and abundance,
> one of freedom and one of expression.

CHAPTER 6

As Good As Anyone

Stars Shining Bright Above Me

Heroes, superstars, idols and icons and all those we look up to play a big part in our world. We have them in sport, we have them in business, we have them in entertainment and we can have them in our own families and friends. We compare failure and success in the context of the people we admire on a day-to-day basis.

> The danger of looking up to people is that,
> as well as giving us something to aspire to,
> they can also diminish our own Self-value system.

We wonder 'Can I ever be as good as…? Or 'he/she is so much better than I ever was.' Or 'it's easy for him/her because...' We use the comparison with the other person's perceived greatness to illustrate and underline our own shortcomings and feed our own sense of being inadequate.

In all walks of life, there are those we learn to admire, sometimes with great justification, but achievement in life is varied so we don't want to set ourselves up for a fall by constantly measuring ourselves against others achievements and coming up short.

There is always somebody richer, faster, braver, more popular. We can use these comparisons against ourselves, forgetting that we are the essence of success, not what we see around us in other individuals, be it superstars or friends.

When we look for something in others
what we really want to see is what we
feel is most lacking in ourselves.

Inevitably our search is a failed exercise, as we forget that those we chose to seek in are just the same as us and bound by the very same criticisms we know too readily.

If you believe that your heroes are more than you are - or ever could be - you can use this as a way of holding your Self back from releasing your own greatness. Heroes too have all the common frailties that we all bear witness to. That's why it is so sad and captivating to witness the falling from grace of the once great and esteemed.

Famous people will have famous shattered dreams but in essence the Self-destruction of these superstars that we witness in the media is nothing more than the Self-destruction we are all capable of played out in a very public way.

Fame and fortune does not exclude
anybody from want and personal need.

The human condition is just that and regardless of status or state the requirements remain constant. The decision-making process and the lack of Self-belief are consistent, regardless of domain or status. Every one of us is human.

Frailty and vulnerability are as much a part of the superstar's life as our own. Use that knowledge as an inspiration in knowing that even great heroes have Self-doubt sometimes.

Take ownership of your own success and
don't just hold the view of other people's
greatness. Own your own successful story.

We've already talked about charisma. Similarly, those we admire all have something that comes from within – acting ability, physical beauty, brilliance in sports, a beautiful voice, business acumen - and this is manifested in the greatness they achieve. They also have something else in common with each other and with everyone else and that is human frailty.

As we look at other people's lives and then judge our own it is vitally important to be aware that everybody - good, bad or indifferent - has a sense of their own vulnerability. Real achievement is dealing with life and with the frailty that is part of being who you are.

> Real achievement is recognising that every one of us has weaknesses but can also choose the willingness to change that is the key to unlocking a successful future.

The willingness is where the answer lies, the willingness to want to live in a more successful space.

Remember, success has a natural home in your heart. Be willing to look for and find it.

It Could be You

Come to the realisation that each and every one of us has the potential to be the successful person we admire, read about or see on our TV screens if that is what we really want or that is to be our journey.

> Have no doubt about it, you can be the superstar you want to be, but just keep reminding your Self to take ownership of what you want.

The world teaches us about limitation and far too often the limitation becomes the essence of who we are. By believing in a non-limited Self, you take away the barriers to truth. You learned from the earliest of ages that two and two is four and that rules are always set in stone. Sometimes in life two and two is not four and sometimes the rules change.

Belief defines the real rules of life. Use this knowledge to support your confidence in your own ability and your own Self-achievement. Be inspired by the greatness of the unbelievable. The real superstars are often the ones who choose to defy the rule of 'I can't' and replace it with 'I can'.

Do not confuse happiness with fame. There is no need to use the success and fame you witness as a reminder of how failed you think your life or your career has been.

> Success is always a relative state and
> measured on an individual basis.

It's very important not to get caught in that trap of Self-deception whereby you look around and see a world that's full of success and then look at what you perceive as your own failed endeavours. This is not so.

Remember that nothing is beyond you. So can anything really exceed your own willingness to be true to your own Self and the dreams that that Self wants to achieve? The answer is no. Regardless of what you witness, you must remember to refuse to change your mind about your Self and about your own inheritance of successfulness.

> Owning your own life in all respects
> is real superstardom.

Do not decide against your Self but rather decide for your Self, for your future and for the life you can live. Be prepared to just give your Self that break and to stop being quite so hard in comparisons and views of the world around you. Let go all of the old values of limitation and really see a world where you can decide so much more and be so much happier in the knowledge that achievement is just waiting for you at every twist and turn.

There is no need to complicate your world with comparisons or doubt. The essence of your success is eternal and therefore it is also Now. Now is your time, your time to be the You you didn't think existed; the You that was forgotten but never actually gone. Wake up to the dawn of what you can be and realise it's there waiting for you.

You can very easily make a decision to forget the inherent right to be who you want to be. What you need is a greater willingness to remember. Your willingness to remember will bring you back to your reality again. What you're doing is accepting the truth: the truth of your inheritance, the truth of your ability and the truth of being that flagship of success in whatever area you so desire.

I am so I can.

You're a Hero Too

We live in a world where it's hard to be perceived as a success, where being wealthy necessitates enormous amounts of money, where being good in sport necessitates huge acclaim and fame. This in turn can become an attack on the truth of who you really are. When you place heroes on a pedestal, above you, what you're really doing is denying a big part of your Self.

> Admire others, acknowledge and celebrate
> their achievements, but don't defeat your
> Self in the process.

It's far too easy to live exclusively in a world of comparisons and far too easy to forget just exactly who you are. Don't be afraid to give your Self a pat on the back in the kindness and knowledge that most heroes are just like you.

See your Self on an equal par. Admiration doesn't imply inferiority. Your equality becomes your vision. That vision of your Self ultimately becomes the You that you can be. As you now know, you own your future in equal measure as you own your past.

> You cannot change the past but you still
> have the power to decide upon the future.
> Use this power, not as an opponent to your
> own worth, but an ally in the making of your
> Self and the dreams you desire.

Rather than using heroes to lose sight of your true Self, the recognition of who and what you can be reminds you of the truth about your Self.

Everyone has their own hero status.

Rediscover and relive it in all that you are. Make your Self your own hero in your own journey, in your education and in the way you view the world, remembering to be the You you want to be and can be.

Look at it calmly and logically and see for yourself the opportunities that present to you within your circumstances. Embrace those opportunities. Take them forward and make your Self the king or queen of your own world. Do not lose sight of your own possibilities, of your own dreams, of your own desires.

It is so nice to have a value on your own worth and have some sense of shining that light of truth on your world, illuminating the real You. It is this illumination that we recognise and admire in others. It is this light that instinctively draws us to those we admire. The switch for this light comes from the belief in being fair with your Self and in having even the smallest of willingness to see the world with that degree of difference.

That small difference gives us the edge to begin the journey of development and begin the turning on of the light of greatness, fun and excitement.

See the Truth

Remember that most of what the future sees is the illusion of success and be aware of what that illusion means in the context of media and the way it's portrayed. This has very little to do with the truth and who you want to be your Self. Keep to the program of what we all know is real. It's not about cars, houses, skill, ability or the apparent trappings of wealth.

Real wealth is the freedom you feel in
knowing your own power to determine
your own world, at a pace that is yours.

There is no freedom in illusions or pretending. I knew a guy who was extremely successful but saw himself as a fraud. He constantly lived with the fear that somehow, someday he would be exposed and his knowledge and expertise would be like the story of the Emperor's new clothes. His success was also his vulnerability because the one thing missing was his belief. He did not believe that he actually deserved the high profile and position of respect that he now held. So, instead of enjoying his life in the security of knowing his own worth, he lived by looking over his shoulder waiting for someone somewhere to call him a fraud.

At the end of the day, life is a mindset. It is from this mindset that you make your choices. The only freedom is really in the truth of what you can be and in an honest acknowledgement that you deserve the ownership of your own happiness, remembering that it all starts in the mind.

After that it's a process of deciphering what is real. Real is not seeing your Self as a fraud or undeserving. Real is the acknowledgement that whatever you wish to achieve, you will achieve from that space within first and not from anywhere outside.

Coming to terms with the real you involves a little willingness to see the unreal or the sad you for what it is. Nobody was born a failure. Nobody was born a screw up. Now you're looking to come to a place where quite simply you begin to give your Self a chance and once again that starts by being willing to look at how you view the world around you and how you see your Self in it. Ask 'am I a failure?' (I wasn't born a failure) or 'am I a success?' (Success is my right). The choice is yours and the decision is simple. Own it, live it and now decide you are going to be it.

> What you're really doing is going back to
> where you started… born successful.

Doing this gives you a great platform to go forward and a great platform to focus on the changes you want to make, on your decision making, on how that's going to influence your day-to-day existence, on what choices you desire and what choices you want. Start with the simple stuff and make one change at a time to the areas of your life that you're most unhappy with. Now, armed with the knowledge that you are not trapped or fraudulent or vulnerable, you can move on. None of your choices are founded in illusionary heroes or a delusionary Self and you can start to make decisions based on a grounded balance of the reality of who you are.

> I am and can be everything I want to be.
> I knew I was a success long before
> I thought I was a failure.

Start Where You Are

So wherever you are now becomes your starting point. This gives you a new horizon, a new outlook, a new way, having seen the potential to be and to experience who you want to be and what you want to achieve. It doesn't matter how much bad the past has to offer; park it and move on. Direct your future in the manner that you want. It is after all, your future.

> Make it the future you would want to
> give your Self if you were a child again.

Make this the start of looking around you in honesty, in hope and in the knowledge that success is now there for you to experience in any form you want; work, career, love, family - whatever you decide on, choose it and make it happen.

Even the idols of fame and fortune have to look within to find a true value system and a true worth for the journey that becomes their life, endorsing the belief that it's not just circumstances that make you who you are. So be aware that it's not only material opportunity that affords you the personal opportunity to be successful.

We all need people to admire and we all have those we look up to. There is nothing wrong in admiring anybody or their achievements but be aware of how frail and fragile human nature is and how simple influences are there for us all as we plot a course and plan our life's journey.

The way you see your Self influences
the world you form about you.

So, with humour, insight and awareness, guide your Self on a course that treats you to the opportunity of a truly rewarding life, where all your endeavours come from a willingness to be the best You you can be.

CHAPTER 7

No Excuse

Who's to Blame?

If you view your life's journey as a process of formation with the goal of being the most complete person you can be, you then begin to understand some of the difficulties that are presented in your path of Self-discovery. It is not only the unattainable that can leave you feeling hopeless, but also that feeling of sheer desperateness as you look on your life as a system that keeps you trapped.

By looking at the world around you, you form the judgments and ideas that make you the person you are and, just like using extreme positives (heroes), you can also use extreme negatives (failures) to determine the way you live and function.

> Being prepared to see beyond the history
> that has formed the You you now know
> is a key component in making sure that the
> You you want is the You you find.

You don't have to be bound by anything, especially not the issues that society would have you believe are sufficient to hold you in a place of non-achievement — race, gender, education, money, family history, social background etc

By blaming external circumstances — or anything that you use in a negative sense to imprison your Self in your current dilemmas — you are endorsing the self-fulfilling prophesy of failure.

Whatever your current situation, holding on to old excuses is just another way of keeping your Self locked in the belief that you cannot be who you truly want to be.

Every one of us has an opportunity to shine. Letting your Self out of the darkness of that self-imposed destiny of unhappiness is what matters. Teach your Self to be. Believe in the principal of your own success and, regardless of the worldly reasons of 'I can't because …' focus your attention now on an attitude of 'I can and I will.'

For many, past experiences of unhappiness keep them grounded in a continuation of that unhappy cycle. We can all sometimes blame the indifference or lack of understanding of others for why we find ourselves in situations that bring us great unhappiness. Then the world becomes a place where it is always somebody else's' fault when we don't get that opportunity/promotion/family/wealth/relationship/body etc we think we deserve. There always seem to be circumstances outside of our own doing that keep us in a circle of unhappiness, fear and failure.

Now, perhaps for the first time, decide to take a real look at the repetitive nature of circumstances, issues and problems that continually appear in your life. Realign your thought system and stop the blame game, which is really the cornerstone of Self-defeat.

Move your focus to one of really embracing your own worth and be determined that, regardless of past circumstances, you can influence and own your own future.

Failure will haunt the hungry heart so make sure that your real desire becomes that of equality for your Self.

Dig Deep

Most of us have repeat patterns in our life. We can become serial failures, all because we choose to hold on certain life experiences and use them as teaching tools to failure.

My friend Susan became a kind of surrogate mother to a young woman called Kate. When she about 10 years old, Kate's natural mother died tragically. Susan helped Kate in all ways possible. She was there for her throughout and Kate loved her as much as she would her own mother. They had a close and caring friendship. Sadly, Susan died suddenly. Kate's experience became one of losing a second mother and her emotion was just like what she experienced when her natural mother left her, that of loss and feeling alone.

On the face of this experience, Kate can see this world as a cruel and unforgiving place where every time she has a degree of security it somehow gets taken away. This is a theme that Kate could easily hold on to as she goes through life, using the continuing sense of loss as a dramatic influence and something she would have in the back of her mind in all her relationships. To avoid the hurt of future loss she may choose never to get that close to anybody ever again. So now in essence what these two sad experiences have taught her is to be guarded and avoid a loving relationship in the future. She can choose this as a negative influence on how she will live out her life.

Or, she can decide to use the loss as a way of learning to believe in her own wellbeing. It's not that she won't be sad. It's not that she won't feel vulnerable and sometimes alone. She can feel all of these emotions - and that's okay too - but out of the tragedy of losing two mother figures she now has an opportunity, difficult as it may seem, to really find the truth of who she is.

> Kate is perfection, success and completion.
> She was born that way.

What she now has to do, regardless of what the world would supposedly teach her, is to look beyond and to tap into the endless resource of Self worth and Self-belief.

In doing so, she can find a whole new Self, which is complete, powerful and secure. And while not diminishing the love and the loss she had felt for both these people, she can now begin the process of understanding the value of Self-love and belief.

This is not the Self-love of the selfish or self-obsessed. This is the Self-belief born out of choosing to see the world from a different angle and perspective, using what was truly a very, very sad experience as a means to develop a newfound security about her Self. This is what Susan really wanted Kate to do; to tap into that inner limitless resourcefulness, to stay keen and aware of what she wants for her Self and to avoid the temptation to remain anchored in the hopeless.

This is often a big, step given our human nature and the human condition of love and loss, but in truth it is the real step of growth. It is where you find that place of most opportunity for your own personal development and successful understanding of who you are and could be. It is here too that you start to see your world from a different vantage point. It is here that you start to teach your Self that you have choices and you can make a difference to your own future.

> Loving your Self is not about forgetting others. It's about understanding your Self and in that understanding you find successful happiness and completion as you begin to see that, as well as having external best friends, you also have an inner best friend; the inner you that's there for your Self with your Self to bring your Self to where you should be.

What you're really doing is building a bridge between you and your Self. You cherish the external relationships with your friends and family. Also cherish the internal relationship of your Self with the You you want to be and so richly deserve to be. In your mind's eye, learn to see your Self as okay, loved and complete.

> Feeling sad is perfectly alright.
> Feeling unloved by your Self is perfectly sad.

And so, we now see an example of how Kate can use her sadness as a stepping-stone to a better place and a place where she has a much greater understanding of and belief in what she is capable of and what, in truth, her two mothers would have wanted for her. Her challenge is to want it for her Self .

I knew Susan well and know without any doubt that Self-success and acceptance are what she wanted for the Kate she so loved. Every one of us has a story of loss. Every one of us has experienced losing something or someone we loved, but equally, we each have the opportunity to reassess our loss and - through the experience of sadness and isolation - to go to that place within ourselves where we are not alone. Out of the apparent tragedy or loss, we begin the nurturing and growth of the true Self, successful in essence, aware and still caring but not bogged down in the symphony of life's losses.

> It is perfectly alright to feel sad or hurt sometimes.
> The real hurt happens when we fail to see the
> opportunity to learn contained in the
> experience that causes those feelings of loss.

Never stay in the sadness that is loss in any form of your life. Don't get stuck in focusing on lost opportunities, lost love, lost relationships. See each and every experience as a stepping-stone, teaching your Self the awareness of who you are and what you can be, firstly for your Self and then, as you share the potential of your own Self value, with those in your world.

Enlightened and shining bright, you bring a giving experience to your Self and others as you now begin to see what you really can be and others begin to witness the true You and not just the sad You, the forgotten You, or the mistaken identity that you may have carried by holding on to a Self from a past of shortcomings in sadness.

Shine as you and the people who love you would want you to. Embrace life and be all you are capable of being.

CHAPTER 8

Truth

Choose Again

Your decision-making processes are your biggest challenge, but now - based on a new understanding of your Self - you can choose to make better decisions. As you suspend old influences, your day-to-day interactions become different and your focus switches to freeing your Self from your past.

If you want to exclusively believe in the past,
then that's where you tend to live.

When you recognise that you are imprisoned by your past, your one remaining freedom is your power of decision-making. We've talked about not making your past the only real influence in your future and the way to do this is quite simple.

Your motivation for tomorrow comes from
today without a dependency on yesterday.
Motivate your Self for your tomorrow.

If all mistakes are in the past then it's time we all woke up to the reality that we can leave them there and not repeat those mistakes one more time. So if you're going to leave your mistakes behind you, make your future responses appropriate to your new reality and not to a perception of your past.

Just because you believed you were a 'failure'
once doesn't mean you always have to be one.

Look at how you form your perceptions and learn to stop and listen as you decide to tap in to a more truthful process of motivation and judgment. Don't be afraid to ask the questions: Why am I doing this? Why am I allowing this to happen? Why am I accepting this?

What's Real?

Understanding and perception can be a most peculiar thing in situations and in life. We all know the story of a group of people in a room listening to somebody speak and each of them leaves with a different interpretation of what was said. It's a very clear illustration of how we form perceptions and what in turn we then make our reality.

The whole process here is one of learning to be less judgmental so that you don't necessarily see your life experiences in the context of success or failure. You see them purely as part of journey in learning that real success is to be found within you. Every day in every way you have plenty of opportunities to learn about how you react, how you function and how you make judgments and subsequently how you form the opinion of who you are.

True success is a measure of your own personal achievement and your own personal sense of success within that, and that's where, long term, it precipitates the truth.

You then have a wide platform and a strong foundation for growing and for enjoying real success. You have tapped into that internal source of your innate success.

Get Out of Your Way

We can all act as huge obstacles to our own success. We repeat our patterns and when we get good at that repeating process we even perfect it. So it's important to remove the obstacles of Self to your own successful endeavours. This is done by the process of not forming judgments, being more open and having greater willingness to see the truth of the situation beyond perception.

> What appears is not always what is and
> Self-criticism and lack of Self-acceptance
> tend to colour our perception of life.

I ordered my usual cappuccino in my local coffee shop one morning but didn't finish it because, that particular day I had already had far too much coffee! The waitress automatically assumed that the coffee was somehow bad or wrong. She immediately took ownership (in a negative way) of the fact that I left half a cappuccino behind me. The coffee was fine. I just didn't want to drink it but her human instinct was to ask 'what's wrong with my service or product?' This is a great example of how we naturally embrace a perceived failure. When we project this into the bigger areas of life the results are bigger ownerships.

> It is very important to identify what your
> sense of success and Self-esteem is attached
> to or dependent on.

Do you feel incomplete unless you're in a relationship? Do you believe you're a failure when you're short of money? Do you beat your Self up if the contract is awarded to another company? Is it a really big deal if you're running late, the customer doesn't drink his coffee or your sister doesn't call you every day?

What can make you feel like a failure?

The simple – and perhaps difficult – truth is that nothing and nobody can 'make' you feel anything, in the very same way as nobody can feel the wind on your face, the sun on your back or the sand between your toes.

Your feelings belong to you. You choose them.

You can use your single status, your lack of money, the lost contract and the unfinished cappuccino (or whatever) as an excuse for why you're not living up to your potential.

You can blame external circumstances and other people all you want, but nothing will change until your attitude does.

You were born successful. That's the bottom line. It doesn't matter what has happened since you were born, the successful You is still there, waiting to be recognised and set free.

The successful You cannot be diminished by what other people think or how the world has treated you

Be less judgmental in the negative of your Self and, when you have dilemmas, decide whether they are going to be prisons or provide an opportunity for learning. You can rise above that war zone, that battlefield and observe and apply as much rightful, non-judgmental thinking as is possible.

The coffee is okay.

You are okay.

I Can See Clearly Now

Success by its essence evokes no conflict. There is huge positive consistency about successful living. We will all recognise ourselves with much greater clarity within a successful life. Failure on the other hand, is clouded and veiled.

Failure is a symptom of your own sense of not belonging or not being part of something and always carries a sense of loss.

If you take away those feelings that fear and failure teach, then in essence fear and failure become meaningless and you have learned to look at life without those historical judgments, to tap into that inner sense of success that is rightfully yours and to use that sense of success as the guide towards your judgment. This means that you don't draw on a history of loss. You draw on the power within and the belief in that power within, not the belief in the inevitable failure of any situation.

As you grow and see your Self in a more successful light your fears start to diminish and your sense of failure also starts to diminish.

So take on life, renewed and purposeful and do not let your past failures stand in the way of your current intention for success.

Your intention determines your reality. Success is not hiding. If there's anything that can't be seen it is the true You, not being seen in the context of the owner of your rightful place, purposeful and accomplished.

You Already Know

There's no fear in true Self-worth. In your inner heart you know that that Self-worth is already there. Give your Self a little trust that you will not fail, because you know that you don't have to. With the acknowledgment of that inner trust you can accomplish your goals quite readily. Just remember, you have to believe in that sense of accomplishment that's ready and waiting for you.

See your dreams complete. See your challenges overcome and then engage in the knowledge of 'what I want to achieve, I can'. Play every hole of golf in your mind and see it in perfection before you hit the first ball. See the next business deal working out exactly as it should.

> Have a perfect life. It's nothing less
> than you deserve.

Move through your world enlightened, without the fear of loss constantly threatening. Be happy in the knowledge that what you now achieve cannot be removed or destroyed because fundamentally you are in a different zone. In this zone keep the idea of 'seek and you will find that success, look and it is there' to the fore. It is there because it is your inherent right and that's the part of your Self that you are getting in touch with.

Remember not to look for problems that are not there. Be aware that, by looking within, you're tapping into an absolutely unlimited resource.

Success follows success and this really happens without any interference, unlike failure which usually tends to be complex. As you start to see more and more good, uplifting and better aspects in all situations, your feelings of success and your feeling and acknowledgment of the successful You become more visible to the world. Not only do you feel it, but the world actually starts to see it.

Success has a universal appeal and so it feeds on itself as you start to grow and shine with that light of the true You firmly turned on.

And now we start to see results.

Look, believe, act.

Make the World Smile

As you acknowledge your Self you really start to see the truth of who You are. You are more purposeful. Now your plan has a form and a realisation that's far more progressive. A new silent language starts from within. This is something that has always been there but, in our busy world and our busy lives, the noise of unsuccessful living can leave us deaf to the inner voice that was always our truth and our right-minded guide.

> The silent language you tap into is the silent language of honesty and integrity, the silent language that is immediately recognised without judgment and has unconditional acceptance, wherever you find it or wherever you witness it.

That's why it is so important to first see the generous qualities in your Self and, as you see them, you live them and as you live them, other people reflect them back to you, building a world where abundance, wealth and happiness are really yours for the asking.

CHAPTER 9

Back to Basics

Listen!

Knowing your Self is important. Dealing with proper Self-knowledge is often an ingredient that is lacking in our attempts to move forward.

We have choices in all that we do and one of those choices is the option to listen. Choosing to listen means choosing to evaluate based on judgments that are without blame and from a place of innocence.

Recognise who You are and accept that
peace and success are your natural birthright.

We are all free to refuse to accept this birthright and in many instances we embrace failure, (through lack of Self-belief) even more readily than we embrace success. Until we take ownership of our own success we are opting to dwell in the harsh world of fear emanating from loss, inconsistency and diminished hope.

Instead, recognise when you start to feel your world withdrawing to that place where gain seems like an impossibility and recovery beyond your reach. At that point begin to acknowledge the frailties you feel and see how they can very easily become the launch pad of the spiral of Self-dissatisfaction and the destruction of your Self-esteem.

Be willing to stop in that moment, for a
moment, and simply say 'I know who I am
and I accept my place and rightful inheritance,
my right to success and my right to be in
control of all aspects of my life.'

You are acknowledging the disappointment and fear but rendering it
ineffective by not giving the situation a masterly control of your thought
processes.

Learn the simple step of going back to basics.
Reboot your thought system only this time,
when you look at your situation, be willing
to broaden your horizon of understanding.

We are All Innocent

See your Self coming from that place of innocence where, in spite of the mistakes you made in the past, you can move forward. You do not carry the theme of guilt with you, but you move forward with a new and invigorated innocence in the realisation that, yes you have made some mistakes, you have on occasion got it wrong, but now you are embracing your willingness to look differently, to evaluate differently and, most importantly, to be non-judgmental in your decision-making.

That becomes the way you will relate to the world, which in turn becomes a really strong foundation on which to build and a really great place to start.

You have a starting point of innocence.

We live in a world of judgment. When we talk about judgment it's not just judgment of other people but also judgment of ourselves, sometimes even the harsh judgment of ourselves.

An example of this was brought home to me personally on a course I attended some time ago. We were asked to say a few words at the introduction phase about what brought us there and what we wanted to do. We had all just met for the first time and knew nothing about each other.

The guy beside me stood up to speak. He was maybe 6'7, he was certainly 19 or 20 stone weight and he announced to the group that he had a history of psychiatric illness, that he had a drink-related problem and that he had sexual problems.

Immediately in my judgment I assumed all sorts of things about this man. I assumed – because he had a history of mental illness – that this man was a psychopath. He said had a problem with drink, so I saw him as an alcoholic. He said he had sexual problems so I labelled him as a pervert, rapist or paedophile.

As the day transpired and as he spoke of his own situation and his own life, I subsequently learned that at a very young age he was wrongfully admitted to psychiatric care. He was an only son. It was in the 60's. His father was elderly and, when he died, his young son became the victim of a family feud over a large farm. As the only child, he stood to inherit this farm, much to the disgust of other family members. A simple way to get him out of the picture was to have him admitted to a psychiatric unit and that could be done on the whims of a doctor. In this instance that's exactly what happened. So here was a guy who was perfectly sane, a young lad of 16 or 17, being admitted to what in reality was a geriatric psychiatric home.

When he was released he now had the tag of being something like the village idiot. His history was now one of psychiatric patient. People feared him. People were nervous around him and he became totally isolated within a small rural community.

Because he felt deep loneliness - nobody wanted to get involved with a guy who now had a history of being in a psychiatric unit, - he started to drink. Eventually his dependency on alcohol became heavier as his isolation grew. The sexual aspect of what he was doing was that he used to buy Playboy-type magazines. I wouldn't say that it was really the biggest offence in the world but he saw it as a problem and a character flaw.

The man was now in his mid 40's and he had started to regain his life but he truly was somebody who had been a victim of judgment by other people. This was really brought home to me as I sat there that day and judged him myself. Here was an innocent young lad who was put away, released, started to drink out of loneliness and spent many, many years after that a victim of judgment.

And on that day, as he told his story, I too had judged him.

> I will never forget, at the end of that weekend,
> he stood before the crowd with his arms
> outstretched like the crucified Christ and said,
> 'to all who have judged me and to my Self,
> my name is John and I am innocent.'

So began the process of him regaining his freedom. As he regained his freedom I also witnessed my regaining of mine because I quickly realised that, in my judging him, there was an innocence too because sometimes circumstances are presented to us and it is only natural that we make those judgments.

It's important to learn the process of letting go and to learn that, even within your judgments (which we will have and which will naturally take place) you don't actually take your Self to task on an ongoing basis and you're not too hard on your Self. Come to the realisation that everybody here is fighting a hard battle and these judgments are just stumbling blocks that you use in not getting in touch with your Self, which is where the essence of who you want to be and where true successful development lies. In business, in relationships and in all aspects of life, that's the place you have to go to; that non-judgmental zone that you have to tap into to rise above conflict going forward.

Retreat!

When interactions take place stay non-judgmental. Stay focused on the inherent success that you are, because that success is the essence of who we all are.

Draw on your inherent success that and
hold on to the fundamental belief that
you are entitled to success.

The rest is just stuff that shrouds your vision as you move forward.

If you find that a sales meeting or any relationship starts to break down or there's a reaction that isn't necessarily the one you wanted, just pull back from it. Pull back from that initial fast-forward judgment-making characteristic that we all carry and just hold it for a second. See the situation more in the essence of what it is in truth.

We all have the 'I'm Okay Factor'.
When you start to realise that, it then
illuminates your ability to focus on success
and that focus very quickly builds as a
stepping-stone, as a process.

It's a way in which you can interact with anybody in any situation without compromise, without short selling your own value system, but rather being true to your inner belief and your own creativity, born out of innocence and inspired by inclusion. Self-denial can be left outside the process and a real feeling of engagement and truthful understanding becomes the norm of your day-to-day existence.

> Replace judgment with a willingness for
> Self-understanding, where the truth of who
> you are is the currency of all communication;
> a communication that is so easily recognised
> and so easily acknowledged that you may
> even ask 'if it's this simple how come I haven't
> done it before?'

You now have an opportunity to make your 'before' your 'today'. With ease and gratitude, expanding your horizons becomes the norm. What may have seemed like impossible endeavours or difficult relationships are quietly faded from your life, leaving you open to experience greatness and completion without having to follow any rule or order other than acknowledging the greatness of who you are in truth.

Unshackled from self-imposed failure, the world portrays the freedom that is the rightful home of all who are prepared to look and accept the perfection of their own creation.

> Unconditionally, you are fine;
> just remember to give your Self a chance.

CHAPTER 10

Release Me Now

Break the Chains

Success is both a beginning and an end.

It's a beginning of how we now can focus on our decision-making and it's an end of what historically we used as the judgmental influences. In many respects, it's a form of rebirth and it really is the process through which we undo the grip of the past in the present and hence we learn to embrace the future.

As you experience this new way of thinking, focusing and making decisions you realise that success is no longer a matter of positive and negative.

> Success involves staying in that state where,
> regardless of the outcome of any situation,
> you still see your Self as successful,
> complete and valued.

In spite of results, you remain consistent and are not swung in a positive/negative pendulum of illusion, based on short-term gain or loss.

Truth is always consistent. There is no loss or gain, just education in the growing of your own understanding. How often have we all heard of what appeared to be difficult situations turning out to be moments of inspiration or turning points? The expression 'it was all for luck' is one we have all used at some point in time.

In every situation you choose how you want to interpret it. Success is never more than a thought away, coming from that place where you find your Self right now.

> The most important thing to remember is that the strength to be whatever you want to be is on your side.

Think Right

Success is ultimately a teaching device, which will demonstrate your ability to think in a more constructive way. By adjusting your perception of the world and the way that you view your day-to-day life, you gain an opportunity to disengage from the confusion that so often fills a person's every day. You can teach your Self how not to be so fearful, how not be so judgmental.

You can accept consistent happiness and success in all aspects of your life because you have now started to learn the freedom of truth that you are perfectly fine no matter what.

Self-completion is an inspiration not just to your Self but to others around you and so you learn to thank your Self for recognising who you really are.

> Your underlying successful nature is not
> always evident, but remember, it's something
> you can never lose

The way you see the world shifts and you start to get a greater concept of what it is to look with freedom in your heart. You quickly learn to get back to the fullness of who you are. And now your resolve is much greater and less fearful against the intrusions of the past that kept you imprisoned in a world where you witnessed failure.

As you learn to focus on the positive aspects of Now, the ownership of mistakes, the parts you got wrong, and the 'it's all my fault' factor of yesterday will automatically start to disappear and then reappear in a new light, not just in meaning but in the influences they carry into a brighter tomorrow.

You're making a fundamental distinction between what's real and what's unreal, between truth and presumption.

Presumption is a world of starts, stops and endings and is based on interpretation rather than on fact. It's a world of winning and losing, of scarcity, of loss, separation and fragmentation and it is learned rather than coming from within.

With the recognition of the truth of who you are - which is success - you dismantle the world of defence that you feel needs to be endlessly justified.

Abundance

The world that you see is a reflection of your own internal network of reference, your ideas, your feelings and your emotions. It's important to look past the Self-concepts you have made through your perception and to focus more on the inner success of who you are. In doing so, your sense of inadequacy and your lack of Self will start to change. No longer will you be totally attracted to the scarcity principle. You will start to recognise the completion of your Self and how this will impact on how you can have a complete life in every respect.

> The essence of who you are is completion,
> so you take a view of the world that starts
> to see a way of sharing rather than a constant
> need to win.

As a result, you become far more open to abundance in all respects. In love, work, sport, the new abundant you, the new successful you is evident and can only shine and succeed.

It is fundamentally important to get in touch with what you feel you really want in life. In this process, you can begin to see your strong points and focus on your strengths rather than your weaknesses. You can then have a process of inclusion rather than separation and you can have success and abundance rather than fear and lack.

There is no scarcity when your thinking
is based on abundance.

You are coming from another point of view and reflecting a thought
system based on truth and knowledge, the truth of who you are and the
beauty of what you can be. This really is a story of liberating your Self from
all the supposed things you may have felt have kept you trapped. Being free
is being you.

With nothing from your past there anchoring you, you can start to
remember the truth of who you are. And now you begin to appreciate that
there is a real alternative. Your goal is becoming clear as you proceed.

You are moving away from uncertainty
and fear and starting to look at the kind
of world that you want for your Self.

Applying the principal of understanding to your life will always make for
success because, in that application and thought process, you stop the fight
against your Self. By doing this, you step outside the loop of self-imposed
failure. You have taught your Self to live in a world of limits when in truth
there are no limits and no limits should apply to you in any walk of life, only
a state of mind where you hold your Self, totally limitless.

Look for the world you want and that
becomes the world you see.

This is a journey where you can teach your Self not to be imprisoned and
where you can learn true expression and freedom.

CHAPTER 11

Now

Accept Success

So this is where you are now: realising that life may not have been everything you ever wanted but also coming to the awareness that, no matter what, you have choices. Whatever shape the world you see is taking now, you have some insight into how to view that world with a degree of difference that can change your day-to-day experience for the better.

Every situation can be used against your Self as you hold on to the doubtfulness of your human nature - everybody naturally assumes the worst – but now you are looking at ways to re evaluate and reassess and not always take ownership of a pre-emptive failure. Now you see the world with greater vision and you give your Self much more distance in your understanding of life.

Even in apparently hopeless situations,
hope in waiting to be found.

Every success stems from being prepared to allow your Self to be successful and free. You are free in the knowledge that your past and present do not have to determine your future. You have the willingness of acceptance that circumstances can change, that things can be different and that fulfilment is yours if the true impetus of desire is present in your heart. It starts with finding your Self and accepting that the glimmer of light within can become the shining being evident to your Self and the world.

And it all starts from your willingness to change.

Balance

Everybody is born a success; no child was ever born a failure. This is a fact I think we can all accept with great ease. The real issue here is that while the essence of what you are is success, the human condition is one of natural neediness. From birth to death we have physical and emotional needs. This is not something we can deny, nor should we, but it is something which we can use to our detriment in the context of our personal development. Excuses are easy to find.

> Becoming focused on the needy and limited
> nature of just being human makes us forget
> to allow our inherent success to shine.

The secret in business, in love, in life is having a balance. It's finding that perfect combination of dealing with life's requirements while at the same time allowing your Self opportunity, allowing your Self success and believing in your own freedom to be everything you can be or everything you deserve to be.

The world is full of negative neediness which revolves around financial crises, health scares and personal safety issues. Every media report is filled with the world turmoil concerns, all giving rise to fear, anxiety and loss. The difficulty arises when your natural neediness spills over to a state of obsession and your world becomes full of doubt and Self want. You can quite easily become anchored and stuck in this space where the world around you seems to be filled with a sense of fear and inevitable loss.

Awareness of your world is one thing. Obsession is another form of existence altogether. When the media proclaims daily disasters it's difficult not to get caught up in crisis heaped upon crisis whereby we adopt a view of a very hopeless and insecure environment.

A measured view of life is so important in the progress and ownership of your own birthright, namely success.

Love Yourself First

The willingness to change can be very easily clouded when all around you see chaos, confusion and global disaster. The fear factor is never more than just below surface level. We can all think of so many things that are so radically wrong in our world on a global scale, even before we go to the microcosm of our own day-to-day existence. My annoyance with the man who takes my parking space pales to insignificance to the fears I might have around global warming. In this context, it can become increasingly difficult to stay in tune with a direction of hope and that's where the balance, belief and understanding become so important.

All you can do is start with your own inner world and work from the inside out.

So if I focus on dealing with what I deem to be my personal issues that then becomes my starting point in the process of correction to finding a better way of living.

For those who wish to change the most important aspect is their own awareness of wanting that change and really embracing the willingness to move on from the repetitive nature of past failures. To answer the question 'what is the willingness?' look firstly at the investment you may have had in your past. Examine your ability to let it go, no matter what, and take on board the bravery of embracing today.

In other words, decide now - maybe for the first time in your life - that you are really going to embrace the future as you may have never done before. When I say embrace, I mean fill your life with the true you, the true you that's not hindered by any past experience or that's not reprimanded by any present fear.

For example, Tom and Jane's relationship was incredibly destructive. Jane was of the belief that the most important thing was to make their marriage work and Tom wanted out. In quiet desperation, they both limped through an existence of scarce tolerance. Tom felt trapped and Jane felt rejected. Tom wanted to break free and Jane wanted to be accepted in love.

The relationship endured in its half-hearted form and in a most self-destructive manner for some time. It became a story of lies, deceit and unhappiness endured by all. Finally, the relationship ended but the lasting lesson was there for them both if they could see the real situation and have the willingness to learn from what was, on the face of it, a relationship disaster.

For Tom, who wanted to get out of this situation, he was now free from the untruthful way he had lived. For Jane, who wanted to hold on to Tom and their marriage, her Self worth could commence reconstruction. As Tom deceived Jane he really deceived himself and as Jane accepted her life in this story she accepted her lack of Self worth. Neither of them was right to tolerate the unacceptable face of love lost. However the classroom for both of them should be that as we are more respectful of ourselves we automatically become more respectful of others. That is to say, if Tom respected his true Self he could not have treated Jane as he did. And if Jane respected her true Self she would not have been in a situation that was an inappropriate way for anyone to live.

This all seems very simple as an outside observer. How often to we solve other peoples' problems with such ease? When your own vested success or failures are at stake, then the ability to rationalise and make concise and clear decisions is not always as easy.

The true moral of stories like these is that we all need to learn the gentle art of respectful Self-love and then embrace the willingness to let it be your life. As you begin the journey of transformation, apply that same respectfulness to each and every aspect of your endeavours, not just in love but in your work, in your family and in all the happenings that make up the world that is yours. As you take stock of where you are, focus on where you want to go.

Be conscious that the opportunity is now and carry with you the knowledge that the power of change is there for everybody.

Hope

You do not have to accept that somehow you are ordained to fail. Accepting failure is the greatest price we can pay in valuing our own Self worth. The message here is one of hope. Have a realisation of your own true value and your own true value will find you. It's not so much that you have to look for it. Finding your own true value has far more to do with accepting and being open to the emergence of the true and valued Self.

I want to be therefore I will be.

The attitude that life can and will be different if you open your Self up to the belief that change is possible comes from Self-trust. No matter what you now accept as the norm, settling for of a life of shortcomings, compromises and disappointments is not how you should live. Identifying with the failed Self is in many ways ultimately a much harder and more trying way to live than identifying with the You of success.

Our attraction to failure is renowned.
Our fear of success is our real failure.

CHAPTER 12

The Cost of Loss

Where Are You?

Very often, our decision-making is influenced by our perception of the consequences of loss. That is to say, using the value we attribute to potential loss as a template for what we do and how we come to our decisions can effect us in a negative way. We learn this system at a very early stage of our development and it is based on the whole idea of action and reaction. In other words, if I do something there is a consequence.

My actions are influenced by the loss I believe I will incur because of those actions: loss of identity, loss of face, loss of love, loss of income, loss of credibility etc. This fear of loss can very easily detract from a more positive outlook and decision-making system. We are all more highly influenced by the fear associated with potential loss than by the right-minded attitude that comes from Self-belief. Our lack of Self-belief causes us to focus on the ownership of potential failure.

Many of us have difficulty being told how wonderful we are because feeling wonderful about ourselves is not something that flows readily.

It is difficult to believe in yourself when your inner feelings and your outer circumstances tell you otherwise.

To this end, the world of self-help books, affirmations, projections, and visualisation can actually work to reinforce our negative beliefs about ourselves.

If you tell me that I'm wonderful when in truth I don't feel wonderful about my Self or my life then I feel even more alien and misunderstood. You set out to compliment me and boost my Self-esteem but I think 'nobody knows what's going on in my life or how bad I feel'. I now have the perfect excuse to once again opt out of embracing the real me within.

It is vital that I acknowledge where I am and the circumstances I'm experiencing. I can then start restructuring my world with an honesty and an acceptance of the frail nature of being human.

> I'm not denying how I really feel about myself and my situation but I'm openly facing up to the fact that where I am now does not have to be where I stay.

All this is done in the knowledge that I can be a better person and live a better life based on finding a true value where loss and fear are not the only influences of how I view the world.

Build Slowly

Building **Self-belief** and **Self-acceptance** can be a slow and growing process, so don't be too hard on your **Self** when apparent setbacks cause **Self-doubt** to return. Again the willingness to believe in a better You is all that matters.

You have ownership of that willingness. Nobody can take that away from you, no matter what circumstances you're in. That willingness is in your heart and the key to access it is in the way you choose to see the world around you.

> Open up to the willingness and the
> change is waiting to happen.

Even in the face of fear and anxiety don't lose your willingness for change. It becomes the architect of your future. However frail, that willingness is the foundation of your tomorrows.

> Remember 'I can want and will have
> the better world I was born to experience.'

Opportunity Knocks

If your belief in your future is veiled by the fear of loss you automatically short-sell yourself in how you live. Countries go to war over loss: loss of security, loss of independence, and loss of resources - the list is endless. Relationships break down because of loss of trust, respect and love. Businesses fail because of loss of income, customers, productivity.

The loss department strongly influences all our lives. What we really do is inhibit our Self-trust as the history of loss teaches us to be critical, fearful and less open to opportunity.

There is a huge difference between opportunity and naivety. You can be fooled by naivety whereas opportunity comes from the process of growth and development. You can embrace opportunity. Naivety is the domain of quick-fix solutions to life-long problems.

In work, love or life itself, focus on the opportunities the world offers to rediscover the successful You within. Sometimes situations will not always appear to be opportunities but in the recognition of where you are in the Now of your own time, there is always an opportunity to grow and learn. Recognising the opportunities in life can be challenging, particularly when we make our decisions based on the template of a pattern of loss.

Past loss can teach us to be fearful of future loss. This can create a very crippling and inhibited vision of the future, where the anticipated shortcomings seem far bigger in our mind than the abundance of opportunity. That's the difference between loss and opportunity.

No situation is a total write-off; every experience teaches something.

Don't let the loss phenomenon become the primary influence whereby we judge others and ourselves. Keep a sense of Self-forgiveness about past experiences.

Having failed or lost once (or twice or many, many times) does not mean that we must accept failure as a life sentence.

Different Perspective

The challenge is to take our willingness to change and transform that into opportunity and an abundant belief system. So whether you're involved in a love affair or a sales meeting, the abundant Self of willingness, hope and reality is far more evident than the limited Self of loss, fear and denial. This becomes the window through which you see the world and the world sees you.

The choice is yours and the results of this choice are always the same: loss or abundance.

By deciding for a better vision of your own world you automatically create a situation to lend itself to that vision. So now the refusal is not a refusal. Now the rejection is not a rejection. Instead the situation we would have always interpreted as loss becomes an opportunity of education leading to change.

These are stepping-stones in the process of discovering the abundance of who we are. The rejection or the refusal now become illustrations of our growth as opposed to another way to demoralise and devalue our own Self-worth leaving is feeling trapped in failure and loss. Now we have alternative examples to inspire us to the greatness of change.

We are looking at the world with a different perspective, the perspective of Self-worth. We are free from loss in the belief that all things teach us the true meaning of who we really are, which is born abundantly successful.

Now is All We've Got

The truest form of abundance is where you hold yourself at any given time, that is to say the only time you have is right Now. We can't change the past and the future is only an imagined space of intention. Now is all we have to deal with. This fact does not diminish our awareness of things to come or our memories of things past but Now should not be clouded by either past or future perceptions. By staying focussed on what you are right Now, you can bring a meaning to the true Self you want to know.

We deal with situations as they happen
and we present perfection as best we can
in that space of Now.

The present is where opportunity for honesty and Self-realisation is found. We cannot be more honest with our past, for it has been, and we cannot be more truthful with our future, for it is yet to happen. Now is where the perfection of who you want to be can be displayed.

The choice of what you want for yourself
can only ever be expressed in the present.

That expression does not carry a history and does not need a future. The light of opportunity lives with you in the Now. Seeing it is nothing more than wanting to see it, not influenced by the unsuccessful yesterday or the uneventful tomorrow.

Hold yourself in that space where, whatever you do, you do it in the awareness that right Now you're trying to be the best You you can be. This approach to living can stabilise how you form your world around you. So, whatever your circumstances, you're engaging at a level that is always acceptable to your Self.

As you move through different situations there is a coherence and direction that's non-wavering. Now if you find yourself changing a wheel on the side of the road or competing in the Olympics you're doing both with purposeful intent, all firmly anchored in the Now of who you are.

My friend Mike was good friends with a very famous musician. He went to see him in concert one evening and brought his boss. Mike's boss was a huge fan and really wanted to meet this rock star so they went backstage just before the gig started. Mike was a bit dubious about introducing his boss to this famous musician; after all, what do you say to the guy who has conquered the world musically just before he goes on to play to a crowd of 70,000 people? But his fears were unfounded because it turned out that the superstar went to school with his boss's brother.

The pair spoke easily of mutual acquaintances, old teachers and happenings that were common to their upbringing. After a few minutes of conversation, the superstar was tapped on the shoulder by the stage manager. He said goodbye, went straight on stage and did his rock and roll thing. What most astounded Mike was how this man could switch from a casual conversation about his school days to a world class, world-beating performance in the space of minutes.

So when we talk of staying in the Now, the key is our ability to focus fully on our present task. Not all of us have the opportunity or the inclination to perform in front of 70,000 people but each and every one of us has an opportunity to perform as the person we want to be.

By staying in contact with our real present we are allowing ourselves to remain consistent and not be swayed by the past or a yet-to-happen future.

Now we can have a determination that is not laboured by negative influences one way or another. We are dealing with the situation of Self in the only time we can practice and perfect and readily tap in to the truthfulness of who we are.

As we radiate this message in the Now of our own time, we experience the return to the belief in our Selves and our own capabilities, not overshadowed by our yesterdays but fired up by the vibrancy of learning the true potential of what we can be.

> As I see the world,
> so too shall the world see me.

By accepting responsibility for my life today I begin the process of determining my future for tomorrow. Unhindered, I now begin to take ownership of my life in harmony with my own Self-worth. I put my Self-esteem in a place of non-compromise. So now the control of my own destiny is far more determined by who I want to be in the realisation that right Now I have the power to be the I Am that I want. All of this is coming from that space where I just hold on to the Now and block out what can be often confusing and incoherent signals from my past experiences and my perceptions of the future.

> A real determination is found in the
> reality of the present.

CHAPTER 13

Solved!

One Step from Hell

Alan is a salesman struggling to meet his targets every month. With every perceived 'failure' to measure up his confidence in his selling ability diminishes and falling short becomes his trademark.

Barbara thought she married the love of her life, only to discover that he was a controlling bully. At first she did her best to please him but now her main aim is not to upset him or give him any reason to launch yet another brutal verbal attack and list the many reasons that she is such a bad wife and mother.

Chris has never had any problem earning money but is always stuck. No matter how much income he generates, his expenditure always exceeds it, as life seems to throw up expensive crises that swallow up all the cash and credit he can lay his hands on. He is now deeply in debt and has run out places and people from whom he can borrow money.

Alan, Barbara and Chris are all now feeling 'One Step from Hell'.

They each believe that they are trapped by
their circumstances and can't see a way out
and yet, for these fictitious characters and
for every one of us, the beginning of change
for the better is no more than a thought away.

What's in it For Me?

Looking at the purpose of the position you find yourself in is a real benefit to the enactment of change. In other words, ask your Self 'what purpose does my current situation fulfil and how is this purpose impacting on my own Self-belief and my own integrity? What am I getting out of being broke/alone/afraid/sick? Who am I without my story of being broke/alone/afraid/sick?' This process requires a depth of honesty that many people are not ready, willing or able to give.

If there's a reason you are in a situation that you are not happy with then equally there is a reason and a way you can change. The choice for change is all-important in the course of achieving your own success.

> Recognise that you are 'One Step from Hell'
> and be willing to believe that life can be better.
> Then actively look for better ways to live,
> think and act.

This is a three-part process. It starts with One Step From Hell or recognition. The second step is the movement to First Floor vision or looking at your life with a different perspective. Part three is Ignition, which is the manifestation and starting point of changing your world for the better.

This process is like doing a stock take of your life's situation and circumstances and acknowledging the difficulties, challenges and obstacles. If you do feel like One Step from Hell, then have you got the willingness to want to change and what does that change really mean for you?

Before Alan goes to his next sales meeting, he acknowledges that he is not happy with what's happening and decides 'in the context of my current situation I am going to have a willingness to look at my life differently and in doing so, to look at my self and the role I play within my current situation. Simply am I happy? Am I sad? Am I able to continue? Do I want to continue? Are there any positives to focus on?'

The next time Barbara's husband decides to verbally attack her she can choose not to accept his version of who she is. In doing this she begins to examine the purpose of this relationship - for better for worse, good or bad. She looks at the reasoning behind her staying or leaving or changing this relationship. What's in it for her?

> There are a number of options she can explore but first she must examine what purpose this situation now serves and then she can focus on her desire for difference.

Chris can break the cycle of lack by looking at the history of his lack, studying his non-abundance and being aware of his right for choice. History – including the history of lack - has a tendency to repeat itself. By deciding to honestly acknowledge him Self and his situation Chris can now begin the reconciliation of a life where abundance has failed him.

The simple steps of looking at where he is and in truth deciding for difference become his passport to a whole new world which does not include not having enough or being without.

> In One Step from Hell Chris learns about deciding for change and through this he will see how lack and non-abundance have been his prison.

The First Floor

Having looked at and acknowledged the real truth of our situation we have the opportunity to move to the First Floor. This is where we can see any situation from a different perspective. We decide 'I can change; I can move on, I can explain my position to people in the context of re-evaluating a need for change. I can do nothing and even though I look at what surrounds me I have an option to stay as I am.'

At First Floor level there are always options and opportunities.

The question is now 'how do I transform what I see as a difficulty into an opportunity?' There is no point in engaging in a process without the determination for difference in ones' life and that difference must be apparent in the form of improved circumstances.

If we take the example of Alan the salesman his One Step From Hell moments were those many meetings where the sales didn't happen, where he questioned his career direction and where his ability to deliver results was under threat. He is now recognising some of the issues associated with his career and the feelings that these issues give rise to in his daily life.

By moving to a First Floor thought process he can now focus on simple things such as the product he sells, the market, the demand, the company he works for, why he continues working in this field and any other issues that may be relevant. It is here, at First Floor level, that he can unveil an honest assessment of himself and his circumstances and create a profile of his life/work relationship. In this process he can focus on the difference between an unsuccessful sales meeting and an unsuccessful Self.

Within the truth of starting from that point where he sees himself as successful Alan can begin to honestly evaluate the situations around him, make appropriate decisions and take appropriate action for change. In practical terms, the product he sells might need to be updated. Maybe its failure is a reflection on the marketplace? The company he works for might be working off a system not appropriate for the current financial circumstance. There are endless reasons to examine but with his emphasis on his own successfulness these reasons will soon become apparent as he learns that success in any area is not about self-blame. It's about self-awareness.

From First Floor level Barbara learns about healthy Self-love and realises that she does not have to accept her husband's version of who she is. She views her situation from a better perspective. She can see where she has compromised her Self and what she can do to develop her Self-respect. She accepts that she does not have to take ownership of or responsibility for her husband's opinion of her. She starts to recognise that she is doing her best and to acknowledge her personal right to success and happiness.

Moving to the First Floor Chris begins the empowerment of his own future and sees that it is just as easy to embrace abundance as it is to embrace lack and just as easy to embrace success, as it is failure. By looking from the First Floor, regardless of present circumstances, Chris now has the opportunity to focus differently on the world. Through this different focus new opportunities will become apparent and hence a new abundance can be found. All of this will come from Chris' willingness to see the world differently and fundamentally accept his birthright of success, his birthright of fullness and his birthright of completion.

Ignition

Every situation has a point of Ignition. Ignition is where the interaction begins. So in the context of change - a change of direction in lifestyle, thinking, working or living - we also find a point of Ignition. Igniting the process for change is the beginning of real ownership of your own destiny.

Ignition involves making decisions based on your determination for a better way of living. Your historic 'failures' are no longer your future influences.

With the full knowledge of where they really are and the truth of the situations that surround them, Alan, Barbara and Chris can now look towards the phase of Ignition for change. They can decide on the most appropriate action they can take while maintaining the integrity of their own successful Self.

This integrity and this willingness for change become the map to guide and direct their choice for a future of difference. They can break past patterns and old habits and embrace a future determined by the honesty and direction that comes from the belief in their own Self-success.

Armed with that feeling, which is probably the most powerful and abundant feeling you can have, they can now commence the phase of Ignition. The awareness of this newfound sense of personal integrity and success will lift their experience of the world.

> Success loves success and so the attraction of this honesty will bring opportunities as they separate their sense of Self from the old world of underachievement, victimhood and lack.

Solved!

Don't confuse a failed situation with a failed person. Remember that there is no place for a substitute in your own life. There is only one real You. We all put on different faces in different situations but there is a core perfect You that doesn't change. Within that core you find and nourish the successful Self that you may have compromised by circumstances or situations of difficulty.

> Never give up on yourself -
> because you don't have to.

At the point of Ignition we begin a journey whereupon interaction has a focus coming from that core of Self-expression, honesty and truth. We have nothing to hide, nothing to apologise for and nothing to fear. Ignition is the beginning of the end of intimidation and a sense of loss. Hope is restored through a deep understanding and a total acceptance of 'I am okay'.

By engaging in the process of One Step From Hell (Recognition), First Floor (Better Perspective) and Ignition (Making Change) you start the process of reconnection to the true You; the You who deserves the happiness and success you crave.

> You make your Self more complete and successful.
> You return to the person you always were.
> You simply re-engage with your Self.

It is here that you find all freedom and all the perfection of the perfect You you were born as. You are in tune with your own life, your own success and your own Self.

> In finding your Self you open a world
> where you are seen in the truth of who
> You really are.

CHAPTER 14

The End & The Beginning

See You on Venus

In Chapter 2 I related the story about the special time I spent with my brother a few weeks before his death. On the hill that day, we spoke of business opportunities and the future. I told him about an article I read about how some scientists were of the opinion the atmospheric pressure and conditions on Venus had created mountains of huge diamonds.

We laughed at the idea of mining for diamonds on Venus and returning to Earth with loads of boulder-like sparklers. We spoke of going to a diamond fair and bringing in wheelbarrows full of these brilliant stones and the effect it would have on the diamond dealers present. Yes indeed, we agreed, if ever there was a business opportunity, this could be the one!

I had forgotten about that conversation until several months after his death I came across a card left in a place he knew I wouldn't find for some time. The card simply read

'Thank you for all your help.
Love Rob.
P.S. See you on Venus'

Despite the fact that we were firmly in the presence of death and gripped by the reality of the inevitable my brother could see beyond his present position. He was not engaging in the futility of cancer making his life so much shorter but staying in the place where, with a smile and a wish, I would someday see him on Venus.

Hope becomes the master of our future.
Belief becomes the reality of our hope.

My brother was aware that he had cancer but he was even more aware of him Self as a person. He always smiled and he always remained more than his illness and his circumstances.

We are all so much more than our circumstances.

By giving your Self the opportunity to be what you deserve you open your world to finding the wonderful truth of who you are, the wonderful truth of the success you were born to be, the success you may have forgotten, the success that is still there waiting to show itself to the world from that place of truth that is You.